Race and Planning

Race a
society
Report
assume
dynami
ning?

Dra
this bo
governi
It cons
emphas
tingly
challen
are sen
'fortres
exclusic
pertine

Huw T
Cardiff
Equal
conduc
and pla

Race and Planning

The UK Experience

Huw Thomas

London and New York

First published 2000 in the UK and the USA
by UCL Press
11 New Fetter Lane, London EC4P 4EE

The name of University College London (UCL) is a registered
trade mark used by UCL Press with the consent of the owner.

UCL Press is an imprint of the Taylor & Francis Group

© 2000 Huw Thomas

Typeset in Times by Taylor & Francis Books Ltd
Printed and bound in Great Britain by TJ International Ltd,
Padstow, Cornwall

British Library Cataloguing in Publication Data
A catalogue record for this book is available from the British
Library

Library of Congress Cataloging in Publication Data
A catalog record has been requested for this title

ISBN 1–857–28356–2 (hbk)
ISBN 1–857–28357–0 (pbk)

Contents

Illustrations

Tables

Figures

Preface

It has taken a number of years to write this book. Had it been finished earlier, I have little doubt that it would have contained an apologetic note about lengthy absences in the study; I prefer it this way. It so happens that the book, for all its faults, is the stronger for its long gestation, as my understanding of the sociology and politics of race deepened considerably during the time I have been working on it. I am very grateful to a variety of bodies who supported my research in that period: the Royal Town Planning Institute for commissioning Vijay Krishnarayan and myself to undertake a study, 'Ethnic Minorities and the Planning System', in 1992–3; the Economic and Social Research Council for a research award (held jointly with Sue Brownill, of Oxford Brookes University) on Race Equality and Local Governance in 1994–5; the European Commission for awarding a Marie Curie Training and Mobility Research Fellowship to Francesco Lo Piccolo, to enable him to work with me on *Best Value and Race Equality*, in 1998–9; and, especially, the Nuffield Foundation for a Social Science Fellowship in 1994, during which time I drafted about half the book. The book was completed during a semester of sabbatical leave awarded by Cardiff University, and I thank the university and my colleagues in the Department of City and Regional Planning for making this possible. I would also like to thank the series editor, John Glasson, for suggesting very many years ago, that I write the book, and for waiting patiently thereafter.

Drafts of portions of the book have been word processed by a number of people over the years but the bulk of the early work was done by Maureen Pether at Oxford Brookes, and the late, much missed, Jane Melvin, in Cardiff University. But it was Michelle Roberts at Cardiff who did the final version, pulled everything together and made sure it got done; her help, at a crucial stage, was invaluable (including last-minute assistance from Karen Dickens).

It will be evident that I have enjoyed the support and assistance of a number of people over very many years. Particular thanks are due to my collaborators on a number of research projects directly related to this book: Sue Brownill, Vijay Krishnarayan, Francesco Lo Piccolo, Konnie Razzaque and Tamsin Stirling. I would like to acknowledge the special debt I owe to Rob Imrie, with whom I have worked closely on so many projects over the years; through word and deed, he reminds me of the seriousness, and absurdity, of what we do.

Parts of the book make use of previously published work, most notably parts of Chapter 1, which uses material from my chapter 'Urban renewal, social exclusion and ethnic minorities in Britain' in A. Khakee, P. Somma and H. Thomas (eds), *Urban Renewal, Ethnicity and Social Exclusion in Europe* (Aldershot: Ashgate, 1999), and from V. Krishnarayan and H. Thomas, *Ethnic Minorities and the Planning System* (London: RTPI) and from the introduction to H. Thomas and V. Krishnarayan (eds), *Race Equality and Planning: Policies and Procedures* (Aldershot: Ashgate, 1994). Chapter 2 contains material from H. Thomas, 'Ethnic minorities and the planning system: a study revisited', *Town Planning Review* 68(2): 195–211, 1997.

Chapter 3 contains material from 'Race, public policy and planning in Britain', from *Planning Perspectives* 10: 123–148, Carfax Publishing, Abingdon, Oxfordshire and H. Thomas and V. Krishnarayan, 'Race, disadvantage and policy processes in British planning', *Environment and Planning A* 1994, 26: 1891–1910, Pion Limited, London; and Chapter 4 uses material from Krishnarayan and Thomas and a forthcoming publication in *Planning Practice and Research*, jointly authored with Francesco Lo Piccolo and entitled 'Best Value, Planning and Race Equality'. I am grateful for the permission of copyright holders to use the material and, in Francesco and Vijay's cases, for their permission to use jointly authored material.

Huw Thomas
Cardiff
August 1994

Chapter 1

Introduction

The reason for a book

> It would be a slippery slope of ethnic minorities asking for things, wanting special facilities.
>> (Councillor objecting to a planning application for an eruv, in the London Borough of Barnet; quoted in Cooper (1998: 132))

> The Rastafarians and that lot don't fit in...don't fit in my...look, I'll be honest with you, in a Constable painting they do not fit in. It's as simple as that.
>> (David Evans MP, quoted in the *Guardian*, 5 March 1997, p. 6)

> this book...tells the story of [a] campaign to build an oracle, a structure for the observance of her faith, in her back garden...The scandal provoked by her action came from the fact that in building the oracle...she challenged the prevailing organisation of space in a white racist society.
>> (Cohen 1994: ii)[1]

At the time of writing there is no other book on the subject of race and planning, and to some readers it may not be obvious that this is a gap which needs filling. My initial response to such scepticism would be that after twenty years working within and studying British planning, I am fairly confident that most planners could not confidently identify and discuss the conflicting views stated or hinted at in the quotations above of what contemporary British society is, and should be, and what these mean for planning. Planners are not comfortable discussing race or racism.[2] Some would say that this is because countering racism, and/or promoting race equality, is not a planning matter. It might be held that race, or racism, or racial discrimination (all terms to be discussed later in this chapter and in Chapter 2), are not as directly related to town planning as is, say, urban design. Improving urban design is very much a direct objective of the planning system, in a way in which, it might be suggested, eradicating racial discrimination is not. That is not to say that planners should *tolerate* discrimination, but simply that its eradication is not a direct policy objective of the planning system. Rather, it is a matter for lawyers or community workers. Consequently, while there may be a place for the occasional paper or lecture enjoining planners to be better citizens of a multi-cultural or multi-racial society (more terms in need of explication) there is hardly a need for a book-length discussion (even a short book such as this one). Loftman and Beazley (1998a), for example, found in their survey of UK planning authorities that:

> Addressing race equality/ethnic minority issues within...Planning departments/divisions *was rated as a relatively low priority by a significant proportion of local authority survey respondents.*
>
> (1998a: 25; their emphasis)

But the comparison between promoting good urban design and combating racial discrimination is not a useful one. For whereas it makes some sense to see the former as a discrete policy objective, as something which can be fenced off, as it were, from the rest of public or private life, the latter cannot be conceived in this way. The choices made, for example, in a school about its curriculum have no relevance to urban design, but both the *manner* in which decisions are made and the *content* of those decisions can promote or retard the eradication of racial discrimination. This is because the idea and practice of racial discrimination or racism, depends upon the notion of 'race' having a social salience: that is, it depends upon 'race' being a social category which is significant in everyday social relations. To anticipate the discussion and terminology of Chapter 2, it depends upon the *racialisation* of social relations; and racialisation is a process which cannot be compartmentalised neatly for the purpose of public policy. Thus what happens in schools, on the street and in planning offices, is all important to combating racial discrimination and disadvantage. The kinds of attitudes and perspectives displayed in the quotations at the head of this chapter do not just form part of the context within which planning operates; they also employ a set of categories with which planners (and others involved in the planning system) may choose to interpret the world.

If we conceive of ourselves, and others, as members of particular racial groups then in doing so, we will be drawing upon a view of the world which does not limit itself to any one aspect of our lives. If we think races are part of the fabric of society (if we hold to what can be termed a racial ideology) then we take races to be part of the whole fabric, not just a section of it. This means the racialisation of society is sustained by its continuing significance in each and every part of social life, including town planning. Conversely, countering racialisation, depends upon its being eradicated in every sphere of social life. So in a sense, race is central to planning, not peripheral to it.

The manner in which racialisation can manifest itself will certainly differ from one social activity to another, and will depend upon the nature of the activity and the people taking a part in it. There is an obvious (and important) practical difference between the racist violence of a football hooligan and the stereotypes which a planning officer may have about various racial or ethnic groups (Gilroy 1993). But there is also an underlying and crucial similarity, namely that both believe that it helps them make sense of the social world if they think of it as populated by discrete races, each with a set of defining characteristics. This belief in the relevance of a racial ideology will be sustained or challenged in the *whole* life experience of the football hooligan and the planner, not simply by life on the terraces or in the office. Moreover, their sharing this belief will influence their responses to each other: racist hooliganism may be condemned, for example, as intolerance of difference without questioning how that difference is being constructed in the first place. In turn, the belief will manifest itself in more or less subtle ways in all aspects of their lives, some of which may clearly be illegal (such as racist assaults), some of which may be much more subtle (such as a continuing unease in dealing with members of 'different racial groups', albeit accompanied perhaps by scrupulous efforts to be fair).

This book, then, examines town planing in a racialised society, a society where race is a significant social category, and one which mediates relations between individuals and each other and between individuals and institutions. It will ask whether planning policies are informed by a critical awareness of racial ideologies and whether planning processes are sensitive to the possibility of discrimination and racism. In short, it will ask how planning fits into a society where 'race relations' are endlessly topical and potentially explosive.

Chapter 2 will expand upon the key ideas, which will inform the book's analysis. In particular, it will discuss the terms 'race', 'racialisation' and 'ethnicity' and the role of space in defining racial and ethnic boundaries. It will also set out a view of the planning system as consisting of a number of policy processes, suggesting that this may help us analyse at least some of the ways in which racially based disadvantage can be underpinned, and countered, within and through planning.

The theoretical understanding which underpins this book eschews the view that there is any specific mapping of 'race' (or ethnicity) which can be undertaken independently of the way in which these categories are constructed, and observed to be constructed, in social life. Yet racism and racial inequality is a part of British life, and the planning process is not insulated from it. The lives of individuals, and the opportunities afforded them, are influenced in part by their being regarded as being members of a particular racial group. More positively, perhaps, for a number of people a strong sense of ethnic identity is an important part of their lives; often, the ethnic identity they develop is shaped by the racial hostility they come up against. At its most obvious, one response to racist hostility is to value the racialised identity as an oppositional strategy (Lopez and Hasso 1998). It is important, then, that the book's discussion of planning in a racialised society is prefaced by an account of the demography of Britain and a review of the economic and social consequences of racism and discrimination. There are by now a number of excellent reviews of those topics and this chapter will confine itself to a very brief summary.[3] It will concentrate on racial and ethnic diversity, the distribution of ethnic or racial groups by ages, sex and geography, residential segregation and the employment characteristics of various ethnic groups in Britain.

The black and ethnic minority population of Britain

There have been periodic influxes of migrants to Britain for many centuries, and although most of these have been from other European countries (notably Ireland), it is also the case that the country has long-established non-white minority ethnic populations.[4] The pace of immigration, particularly of non-white people, picked up in the year following the Second World War, not least because of British government policies encouraging immigration to fill public sector jobs (Solomos 1993). However, from the immediate postwar period onward, there has been a consistent racialisation of immigration in British politics in the sense that non-white immigration has been portrayed as problematic (Solomos 1993; Spencer 1998). From the 1950s there have been influential voices calling for control of non-white immigration, and from the 1960s legal controls have indeed become increasingly tight, with a consequent fall in the numbers of immigrants. This will be discussed more fully in Chapter 3.

The 1991 Census was the first to asks questions about ethnicity, and its findings will be used as a basis for discussing the ethnic minority population in the mid 1990s. There was a considerable discussion (and testing) of an appropriate question (or set of questions) in preceding years (Bulmer 1996), and widespread acknowledgement that the question eventually used was sociologically imprecise and represented a political compromise (using the term in the broadest sense). As Peach (1996b: 5–6) commented, in a passage worth quoting at length:

> While birthplace is an unambiguous category, ethnic identity is more mercurial. Critically, ethnicity, is contextual rather than absolute. One may be Welsh in England, British in Germany, European in Thailand, White in Africa. A person may be Afro-Caribbean by descent but British by upbringing so that his or her census category might be either

Black-Caribbean or Black-Other. Similarly, a person may be an East African Asian, an Indian, a Sikh or Ramgarhia. Thus ethnicity is a situational rather than an independent category. The Census Quality Validation has indicated confusion about which category to claim, especially for those of mixed ethnic background.

The ten main ethnic categories produced by the 1991 census are not unambiguous. The emphasis in the classification is on categorising the non-European minority groups, while aggregating the European population into a single White group. Taking the categories in the order in which they appear in the census, White is not an ethnic group but a racial designation; it conflates all European identities and more besides. Black-Caribbean is complicated by the uncertainty as to whether those who wrote themselves into the census as 'Black British'...should have been included in this category rather than Black-Other. Within the Black-Caribbean group there is clearly a racial designation, but it hides a great range of national and ethnic identities within it and does not represent a homogeneous group. Black-Other is similarly a residual category, containing not only second generation Afro-Caribbeans, but also African-Americans (significant in the geography of military bases) and old established dockland ethnic minorities in Liverpool, Cardiff and other places...Indian as a category represents nationality as much as ethnicity. There are very significant differences within the group according to religion, language and place of origin...Bangladeshi is perhaps the least ambiguous of the groups, with a high proportion originating from the Sylhet District in the north east of the country...The Chinese are drawn from Hong Kong, Singapore, Vietnam and Taiwan as well as from the People's Republic itself...Other-Asians are another residual category containing the Japanese, Malaysians and a myriad of small groups...Other-Other is perhaps the most ambiguous of all groups, although Middle Easterners figure prominently within it. Finally, the Irish pose a significant problem of identification. There was no Irish ethnic question on the census and birthplace has additional problems of interpretation in this case as two very different traditions are involved for the 'born in Ireland' category...

These comments would be enough in themselves to alert us to the complexity of interpreting census results. But in relation to ethnicity there is an additional problem caused by under enumeration (Simpson 1996). In brief, the overall response rate to the census was 97.8 per cent, but the level of response 'was significantly lower among young children, young adults and very elderly people, in particular among men aged 20–34 in city districts' (Simpson 1996: 63). These deficiencies were more significant for some ethnic groups than others. On the basis of comparison of 1991 census returns with other data sources (including analyses of earlier censuses),

Simpson (1996: 76) argues that it is likely that there is a 'serious underestimate' of the numbers of ethnic minority group children, and that there was also disproportionate under-enumeration of ethnic minority adults aged 15–34 (though the size of this effect is unquantifiable).

The 1991 Census must be interpreted cautiously, therefore, even as a snapshot of the ethnic composition of Britain. In this section, its findings will be used simply to provide a very broad picture of what calling Britain a multi-ethnic or multi-racial country might mean.

Table 1.1 shows the ethnic breakdown of the population, in broad terms, in 1991, with Table 1.2 providing an estimate of the growth of the larger minority ethnic groups in the post-war period. Owen (1996) estimates – on the basis of incomplete data – that the ethnic minority population of Great Britain has increased from about 886,000 in 1966; as Peach (1996b) points out, though minority ethnic groups remain a small proportion of the total population, their rate of growth has been relatively fast.

Two other broad generalisations can be made on the basis of census data. First, in certain respects the white population is quite different from the ethnic minority population, more or less taken as a whole. Second, the ethnic minority population is by no means homogenous, and there appear to be significant variations *between* minority ethnic groups in relation to some socio-economic characteristics.

Perhaps two of the most significant ways (for planners) in which ethnic minority groups, in general, differ from the (white) ethnic majority are (1) the distribution of their populations by age, and (2) their spatial distribution. Age/sex pyramids for selected ethnic groups make apparent the relative youth of all 'non-white' ethnic groups (though their pyramids are by no means uniform) (see Peach 1996b: 12–13). A young population has very distinctive needs – for example, in relation to health and welfare, education

Table 1.1 Population of Great Britain by Census ethnic groups, 1991

White	51,874,000
Black Caribbean	500,000
Black African	212,000
Black Other	178,000
Indian	840,000
Pakistani	477,000
Bangladeshi	163,000
Chinese	157,000
Other Asian	198,000
Other Groups	290,000

Source: 1991 census, as reported in Modood et al. (1997: 13).

Table 1.2 Estimated size and growth of the Caribbean, Indian and Pakistani and Bangladeshi ethnic populations in Great Britain, 1951–91

	West Indian or Caribbean	Indian	Pakistani	Bangladeshi
1951	28,000	31,000	10,000	2,000
1961	210,000	81,000	25,000	6,000
1966	402,000	233,000	64,000	11,000
1971	548,000	375,000	119,000	22,000
1981	545,000	676,000	296,000	65,000
1991	500,000	840,000	477,000	163,000

Source: Peach (1996b: 11).

and recreation – and meeting these needs has land-use implications. So, it is plausible to suggest that the ethnic minority population has a special interest in public policies (including planning policies) which have a bearing on issues such as health and welfare, education and recreation.

Tables 1.3 and 1.4 illustrate the differences in the geographical distribution of the British population in 1991. The ethnic minority population is concentrated in England: and within England, in very few regions. In addition the ethnic minority population is concentrated in large urban areas, and is over-represented in what Owen (1995) has termed 'declining industrial centres'. This concentration is repeated at smaller spatial scales, where a degree of residential segregation by ethnicity is apparent. Peach (1996a, 1996b) points out that nowhere in Britain is there to be found residential segregation of the kind experienced 'almost uniformly' by African-Americans, but at the micro-level, very high degrees of segregation may exist: a survey by Bolton Metropolitan Borough Council – with an admittedly low response rate – found groups of streets where 80 per cent of residents were from ethnic minorities (Leese and Wareing 1996). Moreover, a degree of ethnic segregation which cannot be explained as a function of class undoubtedly exists. An Index of Dissimilarity represents 'the percentage of the population which would have to shift from its area of residence in order to replicate the distribution of the total population in the city. It has a range from 0 (no segregation) to 100 (total segregation)' (Peach 1996c: 37). On the basis of such an index, the Bangladeshi, Pakistani, Black African and Chinese populations (in that order) appear to be the most segregated (from all other groups) at the fine-grained enumeration district level, while there is some evidence that the Black Caribbean population of Greater London is undergoing a 'progressive dispersal' (Peach 1996b: 124).

Using a different measure of segregation, a measure of the exposure of one group to another, Peach and Rossiter (1996: 126) provides a revealing insight into aspects of the social reality of residential segregation:

> The high degree of Bangladeshi clustering in London means that they have a 24 per cent chance of meeting other Bangladeshis in enumeration districts where they live, although they have twice as great a chance of meeting Whites. Whites in London have only a 1 per cent chance of living in an enumeration district which contains Bangladeshis.

It is important to appreciate the force of Peach's (1996a) comparisons between residential segregation of African-Americans, in particular in the USA and that of ethnic minorities in the UK. He has argued forcefully that the African-American ghetto is different in kind from what is found in the UK, and has suggested that there may be some positive factors at work for some of the concentrations of ethnic minorities found (Dorsett (1998) argues there is some evidence that wealthy South Asians may choose to live

Table 1.3 Ethnic population by standard regions, Great Britain, 1991

Region	Total	Per Cent of Great Britain	Minority	Per Cent of Minority
North	3,026,732	5.5	38,547	1.3
Yorks and Humberside	4,836,524	8.8	214,021	7.1
East Midlands	3,953,372	7.2	187,983	6.2
East Anglia	2,027,004	3.7	43,395	1.4
South East	17,208,264	31.3	1,695,362	56.2
South West	4,609,424	8.4	62,576	2.1
West Midlands	5,150,187	9.4	424,363	14.1
North West	6,243,697	11.4	244,618	8.1
Wales	2,835,073	5.2	41,551	1.4
Scotland	4,998,567	9.1	62,634	2.1
Great Britain	54,888,884	100.0	3,015,050	100.0

Source: Peach (1996b: 11).

Table 1.4 Relative concentration of ethnic minority population in selected metropolitan counties, Great Britain, 1991

	Total	White	Black-Caribbean	Black-African	Black-Other	Indian	Pakistani	Bangladeshi	Chinese
Great Britain	54,888,844	51,873,794	499,964	212,401	178,401	840,255	476,555	162,835	156,938
Greater London	6,679,699	5,333,580	290,968	163,635	80,613	347,091	87,816	85,738	56,579
West Midlands metropolitan county	2,551,671	2,178,149	72,183	4,116	15,176	141,359	88,268	18,074	6,107
Greater Manchester metropolitan county	2,499,441	2,351,239	17,095	5,240	9,202	29,741	49,370	11,445	8,323
West Yorkshire metropolitan county	2,013,693	1,849,562	14,795	2,554	6,552	34,837	80,540	5,978	3,852
Percentage ethnic group in named areas	25.04	22.58	79.01	82.66	62.83	65.82	64.21	74.45	47.70

in areas with higher than average concentrations of South Asians). This evidence certainly supports the case for planning authorities to continually review housing and labour markets in their areas and not simply assume they understand how black and ethnic minorities engage with them (see also Ratcliffe 1998); but even positive choices in favour of segregation may reflect anxiety about racism or, indeed, the existence of racial ideologies or racism among minorities themselves. Where residential segregation by race or ethnicity exists, there is a possibility, even likelihood, of racism and racial disadvantage playing a key part in explaining it, even where market choices are seemingly exercised. Moreover, as Smith (1989) has argued, an acceptance of racial or ethnic segregation as somehow natural is, in effect, an endorsement of a view of society in which racial or ethnic categories figure as primordial elements in explanations of social behaviour.

There are also important gender differences within and between black and ethnic minorities, providing another reason why anyone interested in public policy (including planning) must interrogate, not simply accept, categories such as ethnicity and, in particular, must beware of regarding them as just convenient variables in a social mapping exercise: we need to understand the dynamics of the lives of people (ethnic minorities or anyone else). Nevertheless, it remains a fact that at present it is much more likely for members of ethnic minorities than for white people that they will live in fairly close proximity to members of a minority group, either the same minority groups as themselves or a member of another minority group. Though propinquity does not entail community, it does affect social behaviour (Peach 1996a), and in a different context Naga (1999: 200) has argued that spatial distance contributes to racialised stereotyping and, hence, social distance. In Britain, it is difficult to doubt that a lack of regular visual contact and neighbourly dealings do anything but bolster the unease which many white people have in their dealings with members of the non-white population (Hall 1978).

Turning now to some ways in which the ethnic minority population is itself heterogeneous, a recent authoritative analysis of census data, and a specially commissioned national survey, concluded that:

> On many measures of education, employment, income, housing and health, there is a two or three way split, with Chinese, African-Asian and sometimes Indian people in similar position to whites, Caribbeans some way behind, and Pakistanis and Bangladeshis a long way behind them.
>
> (Modood et al. 1997: 10)

By the way of illustration, Tables 1.5 and 1.6 show the relationship between ethnicity and socio-economic class, for men and women. A number of features are worthy of mention. First, certain ethnic minority groups have

Table 1.5 Ethnic group for men aged 16 or over, by socio-economic class,
Great Britain, 1991

	Economically active	In employ-ment	I	II	III non-manual	III manual	IV	V
Total	73.3	87.4	6.8	27.4	11.5	32.2	16.4	5.7
White	73.2	88.0	6.7	27.6	11.3	32.4	16.3	5.7
Black-Caribbean	80.1	73.8	2.4	14.2	12.2	38.9	23.6	8.7
Black-African	69.0	66.8	14.3	24.5	17.5	17.6	17.3	8.9
Black-Other	81.9	70.5	3.2	24.8	17.2	30.2	17.6	7.1
Indian	78.1	84.9	11.4	27.2	14.4	23.8	18.1	4.0
Pakistani	73.3	68.9	5.9	20.3	13.5	29.9	24.1	6.3
Bangladeshi	72.4	67.3	5.2	8.5	12.9	31.5	35.0	6.8
Chinese	70.1	88.1	17.6	23.3	19.3	29.5	8.0	2.4
Other-Asian	76.2	83.0	15.9	34.3	18.2	16.0	12.3	3.3
Other-Other	75.4	77.7	14.5	30.5	16.1	19.8	14.0	5.1
Irish-born	70.1	84.3	6.9	23.3	7.7	34.3	16.9	10.9

far and away the highest proportions in professional classes: see, for example, the Chinese, Black-African and Indian groups. Second, the proportions of economically active women vary widely, with Pakistani and Bangladeshi women much less likely to be engaged in formal employment than women of other ethnic groups. Among the economically active, the proportions in employment differ between various ethnic groups. Again, for women and (especially) men, Pakistanis and Bangladeshis stand out as having lower rates of employment, while members of the white, Irish-born, Chinese, Indian and (for women) Black-Caribbean groups stand out as having high employment rates. Chinese and South Asian groups have a much higher proportion of their members in self-employment over the age of 16, and 60 per cent of Chinese males in the same age group were either self-employed or employees, in distribution or catering (Peach 1996b: 18). Variations such as these show the dangers of generalising about the impact of any public policy (including planning policies) on ethnic minorities.

Nevertheless, Mason (1995: 51) has commented that: 'A long series of studies of the employment status of members of minority ethnic groups has shown that in general terms they are employed in less skilled jobs, at lower job levels, and are concentrated in particular industrial sectors'. As we have

Table 1.6 Ethnic group for women aged 16 and over, by socio-economic class, Great Britain, 1991

	Economically active	In employ-ment	I	II	III non-manual	III manual	IV	V
Total	49.9	92.1	1.7	25.9	38.3	7.6	18.0	7.9
White	49.7	92.6	1.7	25.9	39.0	7.6	17.8	8.0
Black-Caribbean	66.9	84.1	1.0	30.3	33.7	6.9	19.5	8.5
Black-African	60.1	71.0	3.0	31.8	30.8	5.6	16.9	12.0
Black-Other	62.9	77.9	1.3	25.2	40.6	9.3	19.1	4.6
Indian	55.4	85.3	4.4	20.9	34.9	6.4	29.2	4.1
Pakistani	27.1	65.5	2.7	22.3	34.2	6.5	31.7	2.6
Bangladeshi	21.8	57.6	1.8	22.9	35.8	6.4	26.6	6.4
Chinese	53.1	90.0	7.6	28.5	31.6	13.0	13.9	5.4
Other-Asian	53.9	84.9	6.0	30.7	33.8	7.0	16.6	6.0
Other-Other	53.9	82.5	4.5	30.8	38.4	6.2	15.1	4.9
Irish-born	49.9	92.4	2.6	33.2	26.8	6.3	18.5	12.6

seen, the male members of some minority ethnic groups are exceptions to this generalisation, but there is 'overwhelming evidence' nevertheless 'that discrimination is a continuing and persistent feature of the experience of Britain's citizens of minority ethnic origin' (Mason 1995: 58). Mason summarises the findings of a series of studies from the 1970s to today which have found significant levels of *direct* or deliberate discrimination. However, there is also evidence of widespread *indirect* discrimination, for example where selection criteria for recruitment include elements not essential for all posts, but are applied across the board, and put one or more ethnic group(s) at a systematic disadvantage. Racial discrimination alone cannot explain the complexity of the pattern outlined above, but it remains a significant factor in the lives of people in Britain, a factor which impacts in an especially direct way on those who are discriminated against, but one which also influences the experience of all those living in a society where race (our own, as well as that of others) is deemed a significant social category.

Equal opportunities: definitions and the law

Combating racial discrimination (sometimes referred to as promoting race equality) is often identified as one of the elements of a broad strategy for securing 'equal opportunities', along with countering sexism, disabilism and, perhaps ageism.[5] Understandably, the outlawing of discrimination based on race, sex, disability or whatever is taken to be a key stage in promoting any aspect of equal opportunities. Legislation can provide an effective remedy to at least the grossest, most offensive forms of discrimination (see for example Karn and Phillips 1998) and is, arguably, an important indicator of collective concern about particularly nasty forms of anti-social behaviour. Thus, the achieving of legislation outlawing discrimination against disabled people has been a major goal of disability movements in the UK and elsewhere (Gleeson 1999; Imrie 1996). Britain's first Race Relations Act, outlawing racial discrimination, was passed in 1965, and succeeded by stronger, more comprehensive, legislation in 1968 and 1976. There has been no major revision of the race relations legislation since then, though there have been minor amendments.

Noting a succession of acts of this kind can tempt us into thinking that in relation to the promotion of racial equality things have, as it were, been gradually getting better and better; and that progress will continue indefinitely into the future. Such a conclusion is unwarranted, and some of the assumptions underlying it deploy simplifications of the issues involved in understanding racism and countering it. While it is plausible to suggest that over the last fifty years progress has been made in curbing some of the crudest manifestations of racism in Britain, and that legislation has played an important role in this (Blackstone *et al.* 1998), there remain important areas of public life which are not subject to the Act, including immigration procedures, much of the criminal justice system and police activities (Lester 1998: 25); some of these loopholes will be plugged in the wake of the Macpherson Report (1999a, 1999b) on the police inquiry into the murder of Stephen Lawrence. Yet Sir William Macpherson (1999a: 5) still felt that special attention should be drawn to the existence in the Britain of the 1990s of 'the...existence of a sub-culture of obsessive violence, fuelled by racist prejudice and hatred against black people', while others have pointed out the prevalence of racial stereotypes and racial harassment among children (see for example Spencer 1998: 82). Moreover, the Macpherson Report (1999a: 5) reached the dispiriting conclusion that racial disadvantage is as much a 'fact of current British life' today as it was at the time of the Scarman Report (1981), following unrest in Brixton, London in the early 1980s. There have certainly been changes since the 1960s and 1970s, but one of the important messages of this book (and especially of Chapter 2) is that the nature of racism can change; the term does not refer to a fixed pattern of behaviour or set of attitudes.

Rees and Lambert (1985) expose the deficiencies of what they term the Whig view that the history of public policy is one of unlinear progress, with policy being continuously refined in the light of improvements in knowledge. In the case of race equality, the Whig perspective is particularly implausible. The so-called landmarks (such as legislation) were the result of intense political struggle, the outcome of which was often difficult to predict (Lester 1998). Further, the promotion of race equality by local and central government has waxed and waned according to the political complexion of ruling parties and the pressures put on them (see for example Ball and Solomos 1990). This is why it is important that a discussion of planning in a racialised society is informed not only by a snapshot of current practice, but also by a discussion of the wider politics of race and how race equality has fared in other areas of public policy (see Chapters 3 and 4 of this book).

The Whig perspective also assumes that there is fundamental agreement about what constitutes progress, that what we mean by race equality is itself unambiguous. Yet as Jewson and Mason (1986) point out, equal opportunities is a contested concept, with at least two main competing views of what promoting it involves, based on differing analyses of society: what it is and how it works. What they term the liberal view considers phenomena such as racism to be, in essence, the inflicting of injuries on individuals, injuries which put them at a disadvantage in what we might call the game of life. To be sure, being from a certain social group may put an individual more at risk of racism, but it is at an individual level that racism is suffered, and it is at that level that appropriate compensation or alleviation must be sought. Compensatory and preventive mechanisms will aim to provide individuals who suffer (or are likely to suffer) discrimination the same chances as everyone else and will allow them to compete freely with others. In capitalist liberal democracies like Britain, achieving equal opportunities will focus largely on ensuring that (bureaucratic) procedures of various kinds are in place to minimise distortions in or barriers to fair competition.

A contrasting perspective is termed the radical view of equal opportunities, within which racism is interpreted structurally, as the oppression of one group by another (though the boundaries of groups may be fluid). This conception of the underlying social dynamics of racism supports arguments for the need to address the grievances of individuals, but also seeks action which will remedy the plight of the oppressed group as a whole. Because the injustice which is being addressed is, at root, a collective problem, the equal opportunities policies must aim at a fair distribution of rewards, of *outcomes*, between the relevant groups (men and women, various racialised groups, old and young, and so on). Positive discrimination (known in the USA as affirmative action) might be one option for achieving this end and is favoured within a radical conception of equal opportunities in some circumstances, but is an approach which a liberal perspective finds notoriously difficult to accommodate as it involves imposing a *new* distortion on the competitive process.

The view of equal opportunities underlying race relations legislation in the UK has generally been a liberal one. It is one which acknowledges the possibility of prejudice, bigotry, ignorance, even institutional structures which may be 'out of date', and thereby putting people at a disadvantage. It does not have room for systematic oppression and/or exploitation: for example, for the view that racialisation may be functional for an economic system based ultimately on exploitation of the many by the few (Miles 1989). Still, legislation *is* important, as long as its limitations are acknowledged, and the Race Relations Act, 1976 provides part of the framework within which planning must be undertaken.

Section 19A of the Race Relations Act 1976 states clearly and concisely that: 'It is unlawful for a planning authority to discriminate against a person in carrying out their planning functions'. The act identifies two kinds of discrimination: direct and indirect. The former is defined as treating a person less favourably than another on racial grounds. Examples might include those cases which prompted complaints to the Commission for Racial Equality (CRE), to which it drew attention in a Parliamentary briefing paper prepared in 1986 to support a proposed amendment to the Housing and Planning Bill 1986, which eventually created section 19A:

> The case of an applicant of Indian origin who applied to open an English food restaurant in a detached house in a small village in North Yorkshire. Some members of the local Planning Committee visited residents in the area urging them to object to the proposal on the grounds that 'it would bring Indians into the village and residents would be forced to suffer the smell of Indian food'. The Planning Department had no objections to the proposal on planning grounds and recommended that permission be granted. Despite a positive recommendation the application was rejected twice by the Planning Committee and was finally approved at the third attempt.

Indirect discrimination consists of applying a requirement or condition (for example a particular set of procedures which must be followed) which, although applied equally to persons of all racial groups, is such that a considerably smaller proportion of a particular racial group can comply with it than others; and where the requirement cannot be justified, irrespective of the race of the person to whom it applies. It could be argued that a general informal requirement that third party representations on planning applications be only considered if 'put in writing' (and, by implication, in English) could constitute indirect discrimination, although no such case has been formally investigated. When wide discrepancies in refusal rates occur for applicants of different ethnic groups for apparently similar types of planning application then the possibility of indirect discrimination being at work is a strong one. Such discrepancies in refusal rates have been found in a number of monitoring exercises in the 1980s. For example, Sheffield City

Council (1984) found the rate of refusal for hot food take-away applications in the period 1975/76–1983/84 (sample size, 263 applications) was 61 per cent for Chinese and Asian applicants and 38 per cent for those of other ethnic origins (see Thomas (1994b) for a discussion of this and similar surveys).

The existence of indirect discrimination does not imply that individuals in an organisation are necessarily evil or racists; it does betray an ignorance of real effects of policies and procedures which are being followed. That is why monitoring of impacts of planning policies and procedures on different ethnic or racial groups is so important.

This is a legal definition of indirect discrimination, which is to say that given the current legal framework, that is what 'indirect discrimination' means. It is important for planners (and others) to know what the law says at any one time, but a legal definition does not give a comprehensive account of discrimination and disadvantage. Sir William Macpherson recently conducted an exhaustive inquiry into the police investigation of the death of Stephen Lawrence,[6] and he and his advisers found the following definition of institutional racism to be a useful one in helping them understand how policing practices could be oppressive and unfair to one section of the population, despite there being a large number of police officers (and others associated with the criminal justice system) who strove to be fair:

> For the purposes of our inquiry the concept of institutional racism which we apply consists of:
> The collective failure of an organisation to provide an appropriate and professional service to people because of their colour, culture, or ethnic origin. It can be seen or detected in processes, attitudes and behaviour which amount to discrimination through unwitting prejudice, ignorance, thoughtlessness and racist stereotyping which disadvantage minority ethnic people.
>
> (Macpherson 1999a: 28)

This is a broader definition than that under the current legislation, and moreover it is a notion which is closer to capturing the reality of the day-to-day discrimination and disadvantage which is a result of procedures and processes being based on racialised stereotypes (or simply ignoring certain people).[7] Moreover, it is a notion which the current government is keen to promote, and for this reason alone is one which planning authorities (and those wishing to undertake work for or receive grants from the public sector) might be well advised to take seriously in evaluating their own practices. The challenge for all those associated with planning is to consider how failures of the kind referred to in the Macpherson definition might manifest themselves in planning and then take such a possibility seriously. This means reviewing practices and taking appropriate action, bearing in mind a further paragraph from the report which applies to any organisation, not simply the police service:

> As Dr Oakley points out, the disease cannot be attacked by the organisation involved in isolation. If such racism infests the police its elimination can only be achieved 'by means of a fully developed partnership approach in which the police service works jointly with the minority ethnic communities. How else can mutual confidence and trust be reached?'
>
> (Macpherson 1999a: 28)

Such advice should not appear revolutionary to planners, who have been encouraged for nearly twenty years, to monitor their practices, improve communications with the whole public and take the possibility of discrimination seriously, as we will see in Chapter 4.

Returning for a moment to the complex legal framework on race relations, it is important for a process like planning, which routinely invites comments and representations from the public, that it is unlawful to put pressure on or instruct another person to contravene the Race Relations Act. Racist representations on planning applications or draft policies might well be unlawful therefore. The Royal Town Planning Institute (RTPI) has produced guidance for local planning authorities on how best to deal with representations which are, or might be, racist (RTPI 1996).

In addition, Section 71 of the Race Relations Act states:

> It shall be the duty of every local authority to make appropriate arrangements with a view to securing that their various functions are carried out with due regard to the need...To eliminate unlawful racial discrimination; and to promote equality, and good relations, between persons of different racial groups.

The latter part of this duty in particular is wide-ranging in its scope, but has failed to generate enthusiasm among local authorities (Nanton 1995) and has not been promoted by central government. Nevertheless, it can provide leverage for those working for more activity by local authorities.

The 1976 Act also created a Commission for Racial Equality (CRE), charged with three functions:

a   to enforce the act;
b   to promote equality of opportunity;
c   to report periodically on the review of the legislation to Home Secretary.

In practice, this means that the CRE:

a   acts on behalf of individual complainants (in industrial tribunals, if the case relates to employment and to the relevant Secretary of State, if educational; otherwise, before a court);
b   carries out formal investigations of patterns and practices of discrimination (i.e., looks at how organisations conduct themselves);
c   produces Codes of Practice, primarily in housing and employment;
d   undertakes general promotional work (producing educational material and so on).

At a local level, the CRE works with, and to a large extent through, Race Equality Councils (RECs), though the latter have no statutory basis, are partly funded by local authorities and in general are rooted in local communities (and, thereby, can be rooted in local tensions; see for example Ball 1988; Ben Tovim et al. 1986; Kalka 1991). One would expect any local planning authority which takes seriously its role as a promoter of race equality to attempt to develop a constructive relationship with RECs, though these are shoestring operations and have to juggle their resources (including time) carefully.

While the existence of legislation has been generally regarded as a major step forward in the battle against racism, many have argued that the 1976 Race Relations Act needs an overhaul (CRE 1992; Lester 1998). The Macpherson Report (1999a, 1999b) has given the calls for reviewing the Act fresh impetus, and the Labour Government has committed itself to doing so. However, as was noted earlier in this section, legislation is only one part of a wider strategy, which is needed to combat racism and racially-based injustice. Important as legislation is, it must not be taken to define the extent and nature of racism and discrimination.

Consider, for example the notion of racial discrimination. The 1976 Act provides a definition of discrimination; over time, this has been refined in a series of legal judgements. Many consider that in this process the definition has become too narrow, that is, that clear cases of what most people would regard as injustice or unfairness are not captured by the legal definition, (MacEwen 1994: 362). It may well be that the definition will be amended in time, but the wider point will remain: whatever the legal definition, it is always possible (and indeed likely) that there will be cases of unfairness or injustice which either fall outside the legal construction of discrimination or are unprovable within the legal system. Addressing these kinds of injustice and unfairness depends on remedies other than the law; political and professional action, for example. So knowledge of the race relations law is important for all those involved in planning, but should not be taken as defining the boundaries of a concern for race equality.

Conclusion

This chapter has set out, in somewhat sketchy terms, the elements of what one might call the 'everyday', 'common sense' view of Britain as a multi-racial country: a particular kind of demographic diversity, some evident injustice (a lack of 'equal opportunities') in how certain goods and services (such as housing and jobs) are distributed, and a body of legislation designed to ensure greater equality of opportunity. This is a sensible starting point for a discussion of racism and the promotion of race equality in contemporary Britain. But in this chapter, I have also tried to suggest that such an account is inadequate in important ways, and the remainder of the book will build on this suggestion as it begins to focus on town planning.

The inadequacy referred to revolves around the depoliticised nature of the account offered, with its implications that ideas such as 'racial discrimination', or even 'race' itself, are definable in some universally acceptable, technical sense. For example, important as the law is, we must constantly remind ourselves that its scope (and its intervention) instantiate particular moral and political values, and as such they must be the focus of political concern and struggle (for an elaboration of these views in relation to planning in general, see Imrie and Thomas (1997) and (McAuslan (1980)). Perhaps more unsettling, because more far-reaching, is the suggestion that the very categories of 'race' and 'ethnicity' are, in Peach's (1996b: 5) terms 'contextual rather than absolute'. So, far from being labels which can be pinned on to a pre-existing social reality, terms such as 'white', 'black', 'Asian' and so on, are 'floating signifiers' (Hall 1996), acquiring their meaning in social interactions which are suffused with relations of power. The boundaries of racial categories are not politically innocent, therefore; indeed, the salience of race itself, its degree of prominence as a category in everyday understandings of the world, will be supported by and will reinforce particular relations of power within society. The next chapter provides a fuller discussion of the implications of these ideas.

Notes

1   I recognise that the removal of the offending oracle was spearheaded by a local authority housing department, not a planning department. However, planners, too, manage space, and the question of whether this is done in a (racially) discriminatory way is pertinent to them.
2   On other occasions I have followed the convention of placing quotation marks around 'race', to highlight the fact that the term does not denote some essential characteristic. However, as I am not prepared to litter the page with quotation marks around 'gender', 'disability', 'sexuality' and so on, I have not followed this practice in this book.
3   The starting point for anyone wishing further information must be the volumes analysing *Ethnicity in the 1991 Census* (Coleman and Salt 1996; Peach 1996d; Ratcliffe 1996). The Policy Studies Institute has also published periodic analyses of its own surveys on the minority ethnic population of Britain; the most recent is Modood *et al.* (1997). Other useful reviews of a variety of data are Skellington (1996). In addition, there are more narrowly focused studies, such as Dorsett (1998), Platt and Noble (1999) and Amin and Oppenheim (1992).

4   Hickman and Walter (1997) argue that Irish immigrants have long been subject to (racial) discrimination in Britain; the absence of a question about Irish ethnicity in the 1991 census makes it difficult to generate data on Irish people which are strictly comparable with those presented in this section, but Hickman and Walter (1997) provide ample evidence that Irish people are disadvantaged in housing, employment, education and health and often subject to harassment (including police harassment). Any serious strategy to combat racialised injustice within and through the planning system must take into account the reality of anti-Irish racism.

5   See for example Gilroy (1993). Increasingly, sexuality is also being recognised as a focus for mobilisation to counter discrimination, a development which underlines the significance of political struggle in defining what kinds of discrimination come to be acknowledged as unjust.

6   The inquiry cost an estimated £3m and lasted approximately one year (Macpherson 1999b: Appendix1).

7   The Macpherson Report (1999a: 25–8) contains an interesting discussion of alternative formulations of institutional racism. More striking than the differences in terminology, however, is the reiteration of some key points:

    1 the systematic nature of institutional racism: we are not talking, here, of sporadic events, but of a pattern of discrimination, related to how an activity is organised and undertaken;
    2 that the racism is an organisational effect; individuals within the organisation may, not, themselves, be racists;
    3 that such discrimination is, typically, unwitting (at least on the part of the organisation as a whole).

Chapter 2

Some key ideas in understanding race, ethnicity and planning

Introduction

The discussion of the ethnicity categories used in the 1991 Census hinted at the weaknesses of thinking of ethnicity as defined by some kind of essential core characteristic. This chapter discusses an alternative way of thinking about these ideas, one which understands them as being socially constructed, as defined (and continuously reaffirmed or redefined) in social practices. The chapter will also discuss an approach to understanding the planning system which emphasises the complexity of intertwining decision-making processes within it, and the various ways in which access to (and hence influence over) decision making can be regulated. Such a discussion is important as hitherto discussions of 'planning and ethnicity' or 'planning and race' have been largely untheorised. Typically, they have tended to focus on interactions between the planning system and ethnic or racial groups, the latter being considered as unproblematical categories. Thus Thomas (1994a) cites the results of some ethnic monitoring of the outcomes of development control as an illustration of *prima facie* evidence of racial discrimination operating within the planning system. However, there is no discussion of what the labels deployed in the monitoring procedure actually denote; what does it mean to ask someone if she/he is 'Asian', 'white' or whatever? One product of this theoretical silence was the unremarked and unexplained shift in their terminology of the Royal Town Planning Institute's publications over a ten year period from 'Planning in a Multi-Racial Britain' (1983) to 'Ethnic Minorities in the Planning System' (1993). In the first part of this chapter there is a discussion of what race and ethnicity mean and, in particular, what it means to say that these categories are *socially constructed*. The role of space in the social construction of race and ethnicity is discussed. This part concludes that this book's focus is the implications for planning of operating within a society in which racial categories are created, sustained and mediate in our relations with each other; that is, in which social relations are *racialised*. The planning system will be characterised as being composed of intertwining policy processes, and the chapter's final section discusses what policy processes are and the strengths and limitations of an analysis in which they are central.

Race and ethnicity[1]

In this section arguments are rehearsed against essentialist conceptions of both race and ethnicity, concluding that though the scientific status of the two terms is different, the practical import of examining them theoretically is the same; namely, confirming the necessity of studying how the terms, and ideas denoted by the terms, are used in processes of social exclusion, domination, subordination and social struggle.

Race

An important quality of the language of race or racial ideologies is that the term appears unproblematic, a part of common sense (Smith 1989). However, race *is* a problematical concept simply because it is widely used in popular discourse yet has no value (or, in most circles, respectability) as an explanatory concept in natural or social science. In reviewing the history of the concept, Miles (1989: 30) has emphasised 'the significance of science' in underpinning a variety of practices in which Europeans ascribed distinguishing (often negative) characteristics to non-Europeans ('the Other') by ascribing to them an alleged basis in nature:

> The ideas of 'race' took on a new meaning with the development of science and its application to the natural world and, subsequently and more narrowly, to the social world from the late eighteenth century... From this time, 'race' increasingly came to refer to a biological type of human being, and science purported to demonstrate not only the number and characteristics of each 'race' but also a hierarchical relationship between them.
>
> (Miles 1989: 32)

This notion retains a popular credibility, often based on the view that phenotypical differences (differences which can be seen, such as colour and physiognomy) must have some underlying correlates of biological significance.

Yet, however strongly the belief is held, it has no scientific basis. As a number of scholars have pointed out, the scientific consensus in the light of increasing knowledge of genetics is that there is no utility or meaning in the idea of the human species being sub-divided into 'races' with fixed phenotypical (or genetic) features (see for example Jackson 1987; Miles 1989; Smith 1989; Mason 1986). This is not to deny that phenotypical variation does not have a genetic basis; but, 'the combination of intra-group variation with the polygenic basis of phenotypical difference means that it is not possible to develop a scientifically founded racial classification' (Mason 1986: 7). Moreover, and perhaps even more important in relation to 'common sense' views of race, there is no causal link between phenotypes or genetic make-up and cultural characteristics (again, even geneticists point out that such characteristics have polygenetic sources which draw on a vast pool and combination of genetic bases).

But, even if the idea of 'race' has no scientific substance, it remains the case that it is used in social and political life. Thus Husband (1982b: 19) defines racial ideology as the application of 'race' categories in social contexts with an accompanying attribute of invariable characteristics to category members. However, as he points out, quoting Barzun's description of 'race-thinking', racial ideologies are fluid and diverse:

> In short, race-thinking is a habit. It is not confined to the anthropologists, the historians and publicists who make up systems or preach discrimination; race-thinking occurs whenever someone, in a casual or considered remark, implies the truth of any of the following propositions:
>
> 1 That mankind is divided into unchanging natural types, recognisable by physical features, which are transmitted 'through the blood' and that permit distinctions to be made between 'pure' and 'mixed' races.
> 2 That the mental and moral behaviour of human beings can be related to physical structure, and that knowledge of the structure or the racial label which denotes it provides a satisfactory account of the behaviour.
> 3 That individual personality, ideas, and capacities, as well as national culture, politics, and morals are the products of social entities variously termed race, nation, class, family, whose causative force is clear without further definition or inquiry into the connection between the group and the spiritual 'product'.
>
> These three types of race-thinking naturally merge into one another. Few writers limit themselves to any one type and mankind at large uses all three with equal readiness according to the occasion. The formal rejection of the fallacy in one guise does not protect against its other guises.
>
> (Barzun 1965: 12–14)

'Race', then, is a *social construction*, defined by Jackson and Penrose (1993: 2) as a category which is neither 'natural' or pre-given, nor fixed and unchanging. Racial categories do not identify some essential, unchanging set of human characteristics, some natural kind. It is nevertheless the case that, at any given time, 'folk concepts' of 'races' (Mason 1986: 7) are widely recognised (even though there may be no agreement on exact boundaries of 'folk' classification). This suggests that at any one time they may have *some* referent; often, but not exclusively, some phenotypical features (that is, aspects of appearance). The notion of 'social construction' should not therefore be construed as implying 'arbitrary'. On the contrary, the construction and use of the idea of 'race' is part of social processes of exclusion, and of attempted domination which can and should be examined, explained and exposed. A key concept in undertaking this work is that of *racialisation*, a process whereby the socially constructed category of 'race' (or, more usually, specific constructions of particular racial categories) structures the perceptions and interactions of people – for example, ideas of 'race' enter political or policy discourses – and 'race' thereby becomes an important political symbol or an idea around which mobilisation occurs (Solomos 1993: 1). As Solomos (1993) and others have pointed out, this racialisation may on occasion be implicit, by using cultural or ethnic categories, for example, as surrogates for the real objectives and intent – namely to suggest that social life can be characterised as the interplay of natural kinds into which the human population can be divided.

Racialisation is a social process which includes constructing a (supposed) understanding, a making sense of, the world. It is important to realise, however, that this 'making sense' does not take the form of constructing an internally consistent set of theorems about the social world. Hence, constructions of racial groups by given individuals or sub-cultural groups may be undertaken in ways, or may enshrine principles, which are inconsistent (see for example Nayak 1999). Gabriel (1994: 185) makes the point that institutions – a broad term which he uses to include a variety of social practices such as family life, education and so on – are important sites for producing common sense knowledge of the world. The centrality of the state in regulating and indeed, creating so many of these institutions therefore makes it a key agency in racialisation (or, as Omi and Winant (1994) phrase it, 'racial formation'). Lewis (1998a: 1–2) puts it in a way which emphasises the role of the state, and also the dynamism of the process:

> the identification of groups and social issues as social problems is accompanied by the formation of policies institutions and practices aimed at 'solving' or dealing with these problems, but...once established these policies, institutions and practices reproduce and *rework* the social constructions in new ways.

Lewis has a particular interest in welfare services, but this process is not confined to social welfare. We can distinguish two kinds of phenomenon, here, both of which can involve the construction of racialised social categories. First, there is the impetus to classify and categorise associated with the management of people and social processes: of ordering complexity so that the state can deal with it. This takes various forms; for example, social groups may be given definition as parts of attempts to analyse the nature of social problems (see Lewis 1998a), or may be used as a way of distributing, or rationing, scarce resources. The general point, however, is that, as Ahmad *et al.* (1998: 13) state:

> The state has…a vested interest in managing diversity and constructing 'approved' group identities, partly through establishing official categories as well as through grants and special projects, access to which is controlled through communities fitting into the state criteria…

As they put it, 'fictive unities' (1998: 14) are thereby created, as groups of people strive to fit the classifications constructed by the state. One source of unease about having ethnic/racial categories established has been its potential for fixing and, as it were, naturalising what are essentially socially constructed, historically contingent and fluid categories.

The second general kind of impetus to constructing racialised categories arises within the occupational (or workplace) cultures of state employees. For our purposes an occupational culture will be taken to be 'a set of attitudes, perspectives, norms and values which are prevalent [among a given occupational group] and which shape their understanding of the social world, and their behaviour within it' (Cockroft 1995: 5). The idea that occupations may have distinctive cultures is based on the view that 'work experience is of central importance' in the development of the consciousness and understanding of the world (of those who do work) (Dale 1976: 12). It is important to appreciate, though, that occupations are not sealed from their social context: people are educated, have leisure activities, are reared and so on, generally outside work (and chronologically prior to it). It is plausible to suggest that central aspects of an occupational culture will develop in response to, and as ways of making sense of and coping with, characteristics of a job which are distinctive of it. Other aspects of the occupational culture may simply be transferred, as it were, from everyday culture. This helps explain systematic differences within as well as between occupational groups. Thus, Cockcroft (1995) found no overt racism during his study of police officers in South Wales, a finding he explains by reference to the nature of policing in that area (including in that term, the characteristics of the population being policed); in relation to race, these policemen simply absorbed the opinions and values of the surrounding population. Within planning, there have been suggestions – scholarly and anecdotal – that development control officers have a different view of planning (and of the public) from other planners (McLoughlin 1973). Sometimes, our experience of work is influenced by who we are or are taken to be, and this too may have a systematic influence on responses to work and the development of occupational sub-cultures.

Thus factors like gender, which are significant in our socialisation as individuals, might also be expected to systematically influence our orientation to the set of dominant values within an occupational culture, while cultures themselves will contain, as central components, understandings of gender and other social categories, including race and ethnicity (Collinson 1992).

These are important qualifications, but it remains broadly true that in most jobs widely held occupational cultures do develop, and within them racial ideologies and racial stereotypes may play an important part. The Macpherson Inquiry (Macpherson 1999a: 21ff) pinpointed the significance of the so-called 'canteen culture' of the Metropolitan Police in sustaining an unreflective institutional racism; and, significantly, even black and ethnic minority policemen found it difficult to sustain and practice value systems significantly different from the dominant, racialised ones. As a representative of the Metropolitan Police Service Black Police Association said,

> I say we because there is no marked difference between black and white in the force essentially. We are all consumed by this occupational culture. Some of us may think we rise above it on some occasions, but, generally speaking, we tend to conform to the norms of this occupational culture, which we say is all powerful in shaping our views and perceptions of a particular community.
>
> (quoted in Macpherson 1999a: 25)

It is true that the occupational culture of police services is notoriously strong, and to that extent lessons for other occupations and circumstances must be heavily qualified. However, the passage does convey very powerfully the social reality and influence of occupational cultures. It also illustrates the complex ways in which racialisation can occur: the experience of that particular police officer is of being an 'insider' in a culture which would classify him as the most suspicious kind of outsider were it not for his police uniform.

The terms 'race' and 'ethnicity' are often used interchangeably. This section has provided some theoretical reflections on race; the next considers ethnicity, to the extent that its use may differ from the use of 'race'.

Ethnicity

Yinger (1986) demonstrates the variety of uses to which the notion of ethnicity is put. In the United States, for example, immigrants or descendants of immigrants of sovereign states will define themselves as ethnic groups – such as Filipinos, Swedes and so on – but so too will Hispanics, who come from a variety of historically distinct countries such as Cuba, Puerto Rico and Mexico. He concludes that:

ethnicity has come to refer to anything from a sub-societal group that clearly shares a common descent and cultural background...to persons who share a former citizenship although diverse culturally...to pan-cultural groups of persons of widely different cultural and societal backgrounds who, however, can be identified as 'similar' on the basis of language, race or religion mixed with broadly similar statuses...

(Yinger 1986: 23)

Such a broad and varied use of a term, even assuming that each use actually has a reasonably precise referent, flags up the need for caution in employing it in explanations of social phenomena. To the extent that we need to use it in our analyses, what we mean by the term needs to be clear, while the variety of usage is itself a phenomenon which needs explanation: why might we ascribe ourselves or others particular boundaries for ethnic identity?

Ethnicity certainly has a social scientific acceptability which 'race' lacks. Castles and Miller (1993: 27) contend that 'most social scientists argue...[that ethnicity]...may be understood as a sense of group belonging, based on ideas of common origins, history, culture, experience and values'. Inasmuch as explanations which involve ethnicity as a variable can be construed as simply saying that a certain group of people feels (or felt) that it shared a common culture, heritage and so on, then it is unexceptionable. It certainly contrasts with explanations which involve the notion of 'race', for within racial ideologies race acts as a primordial force, influencing behaviour at a fundamental biological level of which individuals need not be aware. Nevertheless, a formulation of ethnicity such as that of Castles and Miller, while useful as a starting point, can imply an essentialist notion of ethnicity, with groups having mutually exclusive 'cores' of culture, history and so on. It is this essentialist notion of ethnicity which motivates supposed 'tests' of 'primary allegiance' for minority ethnic British people, such as, 'who do you support at cricket, England or India, Pakistan the West Indies/etc...?'. However, in fact, having the sense of group belonging or even being allowed to claim such a sense is not automatic or natural. We also have Yinger's evidence that there can be great variety in the groups people claim to belong to (that is, variety in the boundaries of ethnicity) in particular cases. In a word, ethnic identities are constructed, and can have more or less personal and political significance according to the social and political context in which individuals and groups find themselves. In particular, the 'visible markers' of ethnicity, 'language, culture...may also be used as criteria for exclusion by other groups' (Castles and Miller 1993: 29). And, of course, this concern for ethnic identification can itself be transformed into a type of racism, as Gilroy (1987) has illustrated in relation to the development and propagation of conceptions of Englishness which are designed to exclude non-white immigrants and their British descendants on the implicit grounds

that 'they can never be like us/or we like them'.[2] This racialisation of
ethnicity is widespread in Europe, and helps explain the way in which people
slip from talking about racial groups to ethnic groups. In the UK most non-
academic discussion of ethnic minorities uses the term with some kind of
essentialist sense and for that reason, in this book, the term 'racialised
minorities' is used pretty much interchangeably with 'ethnic minorities'.

Saifullah Khan (1982: 209) has argued that: 'Ethnic identity is not fixed,
constant, nor single stranded, it is flexible and shifting in different levels
according to situation and context and thus it changes collectively over
time'. She illustrates how social context can influence ethnic identity by the
examples of South Asian immigrants of similar backgrounds who found
themselves in different English cities. One group, finding itself in a locality
which allowed little day-to-day contact, in work or domestic life, with non-
Pakistanis tended to define itself as a sub-group (Mirpuri) within the
Pakistani community. The other group, by force of circumstances, interacted
with the local English at work or in the street. 'In this setting,
women...chose to interact with other Asian women (rather than English
women) across fundamental linguistic, religious and cultural boundaries'
(Saifullah Khan 1982: 209). Ethnic identification as Pakistani or Indian, or
even Asian, became significant. Similarly, Magliocco (1998) has illustrated
how an Italian (as opposed to a regional identity, such as Sicilian) identity
was acquired by immigrants to the USA through their interaction with a
'host' population which recognised, and thereby helped construct, only an
Italian national identity. We see here the force of Castles and Miller's obser-
vation that: 'Ethnicity only takes on social and political meaning when it is
linked to processes of boundary drawing between dominant groups and
minorities' (1993: 29).

These illustrations undercut the notion that ethnicity is some kind of
primordial force. But it is also important to appreciate that social construction while not a 'force of nature' is not voluntaristic either; it takes place
within an economic and political context: 'Systems of classification (social
constructions of gender and ethnicity) are reproduced within relations of
power and social organization. People do not simply invent and re-invent
themselves at will' (Bariot et al. 1999: 10).

It is sometimes said that the difference between racial and ethnic classifications is that the former are ascribed to others while the latter are ascribed
to oneself. The discussion of the last section, and of this one, will have
explained some of the attractions of this view, and also its profound deficiencies. First, it recognises that racialised categories in particular are often
most prominently deployed as part of a strategy of stigmatisation. But it
fails to recognise the theoretical significance of the notion of racialised and
ethnic boundaries: that a system of classification of the social world is
thereby created which is all-embracing, for boundaries have two sides. The
racist ascribes a racialised identity to him/herself as much as to another (and

increasingly, for example researchers are scrutinising the typically unexamined category of 'whiteness' which is the unacknowledged other side of the racialised boundary which defines the black 'other' (Brah *et al.* 1999; Jackson 1998b). Second, the idea that race is ascribed to others, while ethnicity is self-ascribed, does acknowledge the way these ideas are bound up with the deployment of power. However, the account is altogether too simplistic in suggesting that one kind of strategy or struggle is somehow typical. The construction of social categories is saturated with relations of power; current relations, desired relations and ideas about what the proper relations of power should be (Moore (1994) talks of 'fantasies of power'). But an account of the construction of social categories must be sensitive to the complex networks of power which are in play in social life, and the equally complex ways categories of race and ethnicity can be implicated in them. Bariot *et al.* (1999: 11) argue that definitions of ethnicity can be willed, imposed or contested, depending upon the circumstances; moreover, ethnic identities may have important roles in consolidating other inequalities – notably gender inequalities – for women who are often viewed as 'carriers' of an ethnicity, a status which can, for example, legitimise collective control of their reproductive behaviour (and, indeed, social behaviour more generally) (Charles and Hintjens 1998).

An emphasis on the social process of ethnic formation, and the complexity of ethnic identity, contrasts with a use of the idea of ethnicity which has become increasingly prominent in the 1980s, namely a 'simple additive model of British cultural diversity as composed of a series of ethnic groups' (Rattansi 1992: 3). Here, ethnicity is defined in cultural terms, each ethnic grouping is assumed to be culturally homogeneous, and society as a whole is taken to consist of homogeneous cultural/ethnic blocks. Such a view can acknowledge social cleavages which cut across ethnicity but present ethnic cleavages as the most significant for individual and group identities. There have been more than echoes of this view in professional planning circles (Griffiths and Amooquaye 1989), and it probably influenced the shift from the use of the term 'race' to 'ethnicity' in RTPI documents, referred to earlier in this book.

The 'additive model' not only ignores the fact that ethnic formation is a social process with socio-political significance; it also ignores, or at best underplays, the significance of bases of identity and culture such as gender, sexuality, class, disability and age which do not just cut across ethnicity, leaving the phenomenon itself essentially unchanged, but shape its every significance and meaning for particular individuals and groups (Anthias 1992; Hall 1992a; Marriott 1996; Blakemore and Boneham 1994; Brown 1999). The disputed view claims that some essential core of particular ethnic identities exist which make labels such as 'Pakistani', 'Muslim' and so on meaningful over time and across other bases of identity. Not only is this view mistaken, inasmuch as there is empirical evidence of the significance of multiple bases of social identity and culture, it is also oppressive. Stuart Hall (1986: 48) has argued with passion against the way in which institutions, often of liberal motivation, work towards black people as a block. They are seen first in the stereotype of their racial and ethnic identity, and only then are they seen as people, individuals, and groups, with a specific social or economic problem. Such oppression can be bolstered by the refusal of those with which a degree of cultural history or tradition is shared to recognise that this 'ethnicity' can be interpreted or experienced in distinctive ways by different kinds of people (Hall 1992). These considerations show the need to reject an essentialist view of ethnicity, one which ignores the ways in which identities are formed (and reformed) though interpretation of multiplicities of experience related not only to 'origins', histories and national 'inheritance', but also (for example) to work, gender and sexuality.

These remarks highlight the way that complex processes can be at work in creating, reinforcing or muting ethnic or racial identities, and there is a significant body of research – often (in the UK) concerned more with gender than ethnicity – which has explored how a systematic materialist analysis may be undertaken of the complex bases of social identity and their variation over space and time. John Urry (1981) explores how a non-arbitrarily defined theoretical space for bases of social identity can be specified; Warde (1988) sets out in more detail how major portions of the approach can be translated into analyses of local social systems (with a particular interest in local politics). Urry's analysis of capitalist societies identifies three spheres in which social identities are constituted and struggles take place, and which are linked in a systematic, non-hierarchical manner, the precise forms of which at any given time can only be discovered by empirical investigation. The metaphor of 'anatomy', which Urry deploys in the title of his book, is well chosen, for his objective is to identify systems, structures and relationships of underlying significance and to thereby guide empirical research without suggesting that the precise profile of a capitalist society at any time or place can somehow be deduced or read from his analysis. The three spheres are the economy, civic society and the state.

With respect to the former, Urry distinguishes between the sphere of production – in which surplus value is created by the application of labour power – and the sphere of circulation in which labour power is purchased by owners of capital and the surplus value created in production is realised. The sphere of circulation, Urry claims (1981: 31) is the material basis for the systematic relationship of, and 'relative autonomy' of, the state and civil society to the economy. In relation to civil society, Urry argues persuasively as follows: it is in the sphere of circulation that labour power is purchased under conditions of formally free and equal exchange. While labour power is an abstract idea, it is embodied in particular individuals; the sphere of circulation therefore requires 'independent individual subjects separated from and free of natural bonds' (Urry 1981: 33). These, he argues, are produced not simply in the sphere of circulation itself but also – and crucially – within civil society. Civil society defined functionally as:

> that set of social practices…in which agents both are constituted as subjects and which presupposes the actions of such subjects – first, in the sphere of circulation directly; second in those local relations within which labour-power is reproduced economically, biologically and culturally; and third, in the resultant class and popular democratic forces.
>
> (Urry 1981: 31)

It contains no particular common characteristics in its social practices: it 'embraces widely divergent practices, from family relations to commodity markets, from trade union organisations to religious bodies' (Urry 1981: 31).

We cannot deduce, *a priori*, the nature of civil society at a given time or in a given place; this will depend upon a variety of factors, notably:

- the uneven spatial development of capitalism (see later), which can create locally specific interactions with social practices associated with pre-capitalist modes of production between existing and new modes of production or existing and new relations or forces of production, and;
- the course of political struggles to date: for example, Urry (1981: 127) argues that the continuing significance of religious identity in civil society can be explained, in Northern Ireland, as a lack of success in achieving, universally, formal equality within the sphere of circulation.

Identities or subjectives constituted in civil society will – *inter alia* – draw upon and interpret experiences in the sphere of production. Social classes, therefore, are products of civil society, and their creation at any given time or place is a contingent matter dependent on the experiences of class struggle, with those related to cleavages based on, for example, gender or race or ethnicity (though the conflict at the point of production between those who have sold their labour power and those who are organising, supervising and managing it is a characteristic of the capitalist mode of production).

To sum up, Urry is concerned to argue against the idea that social identities (including racialised identities) of some kind of primary nature are created solely in the economic sphere (more specifically the sphere of production). On the contrary he argues that:

- even the social identity traditionally theorised as a product of the social relations in production (class) cannot be constituted solely within it, and
- that within civil society different kinds of social identities, or individual subjectives, can be constituted, and these can penetrate and influence

the nature of social relations in production (as will be seen later in relation to the patriarchal nature of social relations in the production
process in certain towns in Lancashire in the early years of the twentieth
century). To this we might add that individuals will find themselves
constituted as subjects with multiple identities (in the sense of at least
more than one), and the salience of particular identities will themselves
depend upon the dynamics of the spheres discussed above, and their
interactions.

In relation to the capitalist state, Urry argues that it is related to the
nature of capital and the changing requirements of the accumulation
process in a minimal sense: 'the capitalist state...possesses a form which is
given by its attempt to sustain the overall conditions under which profitable
accumulation can take place within its territory' (1981: 101). But in
primarily undertaking this task it intervenes in civil society, the focus of the
reproduction of labour power. However, its sensitivity to, through intervention in, civil society sets it up as a target for political action by a variety of
social groups who have demands which may not always be related to the
sphere of reproduction (for example, demands for factory legislation).
Duncan and Goodwin (1988), who follow the broad thrust of Urry's
approach, have explored the significance of the uneven spatial development
of capitalism for the development of the state at local levels. They argue that
the development of the local state is a response to uneven development, in
particular to the uneven development of civil society in which the state intervenes. However, once established, the local state becomes a focus for
political struggle, and its character will in part reflect the nature of significant local social relations, which may include patriarchal relations (and
racialised relations) as well as class relations. The qualification 'in part' is
important because the local state has a relationship to the national state, the
precise nature of which will be a product of history and the current balance
of political forces mobilised locally and nationally, but which will modify
the influence of local politics on local policy making (Warde 1988: 93;
Duncan and Goodwin 1988).
    Broadly following Urry's approach, Warde (1988) makes some very
specific suggestions about how spatial variations in the formation of class,
gender and race or ethnicity may occur. He argues that there are 'three
central material elements of a local social system, the material bases of the
social relations which constitute a "locality", and the foundations of local
political mobilisation' (1988: 90). These are workplace regime, the labour
market and modes of provision for the reproduction of labour power. These
elements are both internally complex and interdependent, being more
detailed specification of Urry's broad categories of the economy and civil
society.
    The notion of 'workplace regime' is based on Burawoy's (1985) work, and

refers to 'the means used to regulate struggles around the relations of domination in any workplace' (Warde 1988: 77). But, following Urry, Warde conceives of the subjects in struggle in the workplace as individuals whose identities are in part fashioned through experiences and struggles in civil society. The major means of articulation of the spheres of production (the workplace) and reproduction in civil society is the sphere of circulation (the labour market, in Warde's case) in which labour power, defined in certain ways, is bought and sold. The definition of the nature of that labour power will depend both upon the pressures and demands of the production process – including the technical aspects of the division of labour – and upon the course of struggles within civil society (for example, struggles over patriarchal domination in the home, which may affect segmentation of the labour market). The workplace struggle and the resultant workplace regime at any time both influences and is influenced by activities of the state, locally and nationally. This occurs because of the state's capacity to intervene in civil society, (as described earlier) with its implications for the reproduction of labour power, and also because it can intervene directly in the regulation of production (such as through factory legislation). The course of the workplace struggle will involve, therefore, a consideration by those involved of the scope for state intervention in support of their objectives and of the methods available to secure such intervention. This is a very plausible and powerful approach to which only one major amendment will be made; some account must be taken of the importance of time in the creation of localities. The precise scale at which the processes Warde highlights operate can vary at any one time, and over time. In relation to the latter, it is unlikely that adjustments in political (or other) behaviour will be instantaneous; on the contrary, there can be significant time lags involved.

As far as urban and planning policy, and its evaluation, is concerned, a key proposition is that urban policy, and the processes involved in its formulation and implementation, will both reflect and help sustain particular group identities and social relations involving them. Analyses such as those of Healey et al. (1988) have illustrated some of the many ways in which groups or individuals can be incorporated into, or excluded from, policy processes, and Katzneltson et al. (1982), using North American case studies, have argued that there can be geographically and historically specific factors which might give rise to certain kinds of group identities rather than others being significant in particular policy areas. They illustrate the way in which race became significant in political struggles around education in the United States, while class was more significant in the UK, a consequence – they argue – of the different ways in which lines of inclusion and exclusion were drawn within educational policy, lines which reflected and reinforced power relations outside education. As Solomos (1993: 31) puts it, in his review of theories of race, 'the process by which race is given particular meanings are variable across and within national boundaries and are shaped by political, legal and socio-economic environments', and Marx (1997) has shown how the construction of racial classifications was central to the social construction of nationhood, but in very different (and historically contingent) ways in Brazil, South Africa and the USA.

The complex interaction of political, institutional and other factors is sketched (if not explored) by Burns *et al.* (1994: 206–9) as part of their account of the decentralisation of local government in Tower Hamlets in the 1980s. They point out that: 'Within Tower Hamlets two forms of democratic structure dominate – the neighbourhood committees and the consultative forums' (1994: 207); 'given the dominance of the white working class within the consultative forums, the Bangladeshi community has little alternative but to seek representation through the formal system of competitive party politics as it is fought out at neighbourhood level' (1994: 208), which gives access to the neighbourhood committees. This strategy, however, involves placing 'the needs of a particular party or spatial community before the needs of the Bangladeshi community in general' (1994: 208). Indeed, it seems to exacerbate political divisions between Bangladeshis, for Bangladeshi councillors are found in both Labour and Liberal parties. Burns *et al.* assume, rather than demonstrate in detail, the way in which Tower Hamlet's Bangladeshis construct their identities, but their argument about the interaction of a variety of factors in hindering or assisting the creation of coherent 'voices' is persuasive.

Similarly, Jeffers *et al.* (1996: 124) 'wish to draw attention to the way in which the allocation of resources by governmental and other organisations may both contribute to the construction of group boundaries and to the development of competition or collaboration across such boundaries'. Even if resources are scarce, competition, (so central to recent British urban policy (Oatley 1998)) is not the only method of allocating them; moreover, even if competition is used as an allocative mechanism, the 'rules of the game' can be constructed in ways which foster co-operation across racialised boundaries and may thereby work (in however modest a way) to their eradication. A further conclusion drawn by Jeffers *et al.* (1996), who studied seven community initiatives in three British cities, is that: 'The starting point for understanding the racialisation of community and other boundaries must be to realise the specificity of the phenomenon. No two localities are alike, and no two neighbourhoods within a locality are alike' (1996: 123). This points to the significance of space in racialisation, and this is what is considered in the next section.

The role of space in constructing categories and identities

The social construction of categories such as race and ethnicity is a spatial phenomenon in two (related) ways. First, the construction of categories or identities involves, simultaneously, the construction of *places*, the latter term referring to the creation of 'physical locations imbued with human meaning' (Cosgrove 1989: 104). Putting the matter crudely, being a certain sort of person (or group) involves some or all of the following:

- using the built and natural environment in a certain way;
- perhaps having the right (legal or customary) to be in certain places and do certain things;
- less tangibly, it means feeling comfortable in certain places, feeling 'at home' or, simply, not ill at ease.

These considerations apply to all social categories, including ethnic and racialised ones.

In relation to the use of space, Taylor *et al.* (1996: 215ff) document the distinctive influences shaping the leisure activities of a number of Asians living in Manchester and Sheffield. Social and religious norms rule out certain kinds of so-called 'mass entertainment' (such as frequenting pubs, or watching certain television programmes or films), and, by default, encourage 'highly segregated and group-protective practices' (Taylor *et al.* 1996: 215), such as visiting Manchester Airport to watch planes take off and land. Similarly, the shopping patterns of ethnic minorities were very distinctive in ways not wholly connected to their level of income – they sought certain kinds of goods (especially foodstuffs) which were only available in certain places. Sometimes these distinctive uses of space are the direct consequence of racism, and Wrench *et al.* (1993: 124) found ethnic minority families in Harlow New Town 'for whom ordinary aspects of life were so oppressive in Harlow that they would travel for two hours to Leicester, a city of long standing Asian population, for their social and community activities and weekly shopping'.

Having a certain ethnic identity is considerably easier to sustain as a lived social reality if there are places in which one can meet others who affirm the same ethnicity; in daily life one sees a range of spaces being used in this way, such as places of worship, places of entertainment, schools (and their related activities), shops and so on. *One* of the important opportunities offered by Irish bars, Italian delicatessens, Welsh-speaking pubs or chapels, Somali mosques and so on can be to provide places for people to meet and reaffirm their ethnic identities. Conversely, people who do not feel themselves to be, and perhaps do not want to be, categorised in a certain way may feel uncomfortable in at least some of these places. Moreover, the lack of such spaces can make it more difficult to sustain certain identities and can spark understandable resentments among those for whom a particular identity, thinking of themselves in a certain way, is important. One of the undercurrents in the long-running saga of the attempt to gain planning permission for changing the use of a residential college in the Hertfordshire countryside, Bhaktivedanta Manor, to a Hare Krishna temple was the clash between a conception of what were appropriate activities in the English countryside (which did not allow for festivals for non-Christian religions), and a need felt by a large proportion of Hindus (mostly, though not exclusively, of Asian origin) to have a special, significant, place to act as a national focus for their religious community.[3] A point made by Glaeser (1998) may also offer insights into the tenacity with which views are held in conflicts such as that over the planning application. He argues that we use space in important ways to present ourselves: we 'do up' our home or our office, we vie for the 'best kept village' award or recognition in a Britain in Bloom competition. The kinds of people seen on 'our' streets, who live in 'our' place, constrains an aspect of our presentation of self.

This example shows vividly how in a racialised society – that is, one where racial categorisation is an important mediator in, and shaper of, social relations – space will also be racialised. A feature of rural racist invective is the accusation that black people 'don't belong' in the countryside (Jay 1992). Of course, similar views and values have long operated in urban areas too, helping to sustain, among other phenomena, the noticeable racial segregation of British cities. In Chapter 3 we will touch upon the mechanisms which can create residential segregation; for the moment, let us recognise the significance of the lack of public comment or outcry about it, the acceptance of its 'naturalness', which itself is an example of the racialisation of space (Smith 1989). It is important to appreciate that in these processes, race and space mutually constitute each other; that is, the nature of the place is defined simultaneously with the social construction of 'race'. The boundaries of race are (partly) defined in terms of who can use, or belong in, certain kinds of spaces. The same point can be made in relation to other socially constructed categories; thus Murdoch and Marsden (1994: 1) assert that: 'Class formation is, at one and the same time, place formation'. And a corollary of this is that place formation, racial formation, class formation and so on occur simultaneously: that racialisation, for example, is simultaneously spatial, gendered and class-related. The leads O'Brien (1998: 19) to conclude that: 'Race and gender are so tightly braided with social class that it is simply not possible to determine whether the relative lack of access to power and privilege is based on economic or categorical differences.' Not all would agree; but, in any event, tightly braided as these processes are, it is still possible to identify inequality and to address its (undoubtedly complex) roots.

The processes being referred to here are continuous; social categories and places are continually confirmed and/or challenged, although of course there are times when the dynamics are more rather than less vigorous, and even occasions of sudden change. Moreover, like all social processes, they are not only suffused with relations of power but are also subject to contestation (which, indeed, may be another way of saying the same thing). Peter

Jackson (1998a: 177) has noted how 'shopping malls and other planned retail developments involve the domestication of public space, reducing the risks of unplanned social encounters'. These are spaces which are both gendered and racialised, inasmuch as (in Britain) for some time it is, for example, encounters with groups of apparently aimless young black men which are among these highest on the list of needing to be 'planned out' (Hall *et al.* 1978). Moreover, even among shopping malls, some are perceived as more middle class and more white than others (Jackson 1998a: 181–7). However, such perceptions and meanings are challenged; young people, for example, through various practices try to create spaces of significance to them (Sibley 1995) and exploit what is available on their terms (Lees 1998).

Planners, whose activities (on any definition of their professional remit) must include intervening in the use of space, cannot afford to ignore these processes. To do so may be to be complicit in sustaining racialisation and the inequalities which flow from it (Forester 1989). Consider an urban regeneration document produced by a Midlands city and submitted as part of its response to a study on ethnic minorities and the planning system commissioned by the RTPI (Krishnarayan and Thomas 1993). The document deals with an inner city area where 16 per cent of the population is made up of ethnic minorities (but 60 per cent of the school population is of such a background). In various exhaustive lists of issues and problems, the 'concentration of…people from an ethnic minority background', and of white elderly people is mentioned, as is the existence of 'negative attitudes towards a multi-cultural society…' and a general lack of social facilities. The document sees the need for a multi-agency approach, and the need for multi-lingual leaflets and discussion with ethnic minority groups. But nowhere in the twenty or so pages of technical report and analysis is there any account of, or feel for, the two social groups who are living side by side with little contact (or perhaps mutual understanding) and with a variety of differing (but perhaps complementary) needs. The worthy procession of projects on environmental improvement, housing improvement, litter picking and so on is divorced in the document from any social or cultural context, especially from the social reality of racialisation of space. For example, why is the distinctive demographic profile emerging? Is it a case of 'white flight'? If so, are the white elderly, who remain, embittered because they cannot 'fly'? Or are they making a positive decision to stay in a place they regard as theirs? Or, indeed, are they indifferent to the social changes in the area? These kinds of questions need to be asked and addressed directly, for they will highlight social and economic inequalities which planning should help address. In addition, they may help the planners devise implementation strategies, by finding answers to questions such as, what kind of sense of place, or pride of place, is there to exploit or bolster?

The silence of the managers and promoters of spatial change about race and racialisation is exemplified by the alternative histories of the Cardiff

Bay area (where major regeneration has been proposed and undertaken) offered by residents and officers of the Cardiff Bay Development Corporation (Open University 1997). For the former, the meaning of their locality is inextricably bound up with its being a haven in a racist city (this is not to romanticise the area's history of poverty, but simply to acknowledge resident perceptions of the relative security of the Butetown/Tiger Bay/Docks Area). The officers of the development corporation ignore the history of racism, and indeed make no mention of contemporary racism in their policies (Thomas *et al.* 1996). But ignoring racialisation (and racism) does not mean it will go away, and can appear to devalue the experience and sense of self of people for whom it is a conscious part of their day-to-day reality.

The second way in which space must be taken into account in understanding the social construction of categories is through an appreciation that social relations (including the precise content of socially constructed categories and identities) vary over space. Capitalism has developed in a spatially uneven way, and in so doing has created spatial variation in built form and infrastructure, and also in social relations.

The starting point is 'the geographically uneven spread of those factors which affect the profitability of production processes' (Bagguley *et al.* 1990: 15). Historically, Duncan and Goodwin (1988) suggest that these may have been predominantly natural resources, the uneven distribution of which will have made production of certain goods more profitable in one location than another. However, in Bagguley et al.'s formulation: 'New rounds of investment will be geographically patterned in response to the pre-existing spatial pattern' (1990 p. 150), or in other words, in searching out opportunities for profitable investment, capitalists will perforce take into account the package of resources/constraints offered by particular geographical locations. These will include not only natural resources (such as mineral deposits) but also the kind of built environment which has been developed (including transport and other infrastructure) and, increasingly, 'human resources' (the skills, aptitudes and attitudes of the available workforce). There is of course no guarantee that places suitable for a certain kind of production will remain the most profitable location, should technologies change (and technological change, for our purposes, can involve not simply advances in science-based technology but also new methods of management or workplace organisation).

This perspective on the spatial dimension of capital accumulation provides a basis for understanding how different locations will contain different mixes and patterns of buildings and physical infrastructure: some of those differences, at least, will relate to different opportunities – and increasingly different opportunities – for profitable investment. However, production involves social relations as well as technologies; factories or offices are organised in particular ways and are staffed by particular groups of people. Moreover, the production process does not exist in a social or economic vacuum; the workforce must be fed, housed, entertained, educated and so on, and there is a process of reproduction of the workforce which will also be organised in a particular way, incorporating technologies and involving particular kinds of social relations. Duncan and Goodwin (1988) stress the significance of the uneven spatial development of capitalism in creating spatially distinct patterns of social relations in the spheres of production and reproduction of the workforce as new rounds of investment interact with existing physical and cultural/social patterns:

> The practices of civil society are constituted contingently, in the context of nature, of each other and of world capitalism. For example, gender divisions of labour in simple gatherer–hunter societies…owe much to the cultural interpretation and organisation of labour…The same principle holds in capitalist societies, except that now the uneven development of capitalism overlaps natural unevenness.
>
> (1988: 69)

However, this spatial variation is 'variation on a theme', and the theme is defined by general structural characteristics of the way society reproduces itself. There may be working-class areas which are more, or less, politically radical and these differences may feed into and reflect differences in working practices, educational and cultural life, even family life. But most enterprises in both kinds of areas will still operate in a recognisably capitalist fashion, and relations between the sexes will, in general, be patriarchal.

Yet, as McDowell and Massey (1984) put it in relation to the effects of capitalist development on inequalities between the sexes what they are:

> arguing is that the contrasting forms of economic development in different parts of the country presented distinct conditions for the maintenance of male dominance. *Extremely* schematically, capitalism presented patriarchy with different challenges in different parts of the country. The question was in what ways the terms of male dominance would be reformulated within these changed conditions. Further, this process of accommodation between capitalism and patriarchy produced a different synthesis of the two in different places. It was a synthesis which was clearly visible in the nature of gender relations, and in the lives of women.
>
> (1984: 128)

And, we might add, in the nature of local politics. Mark-Lawson and Warde (1987) trace examples of the locally specific connections between social relations in the process of production, the domestic sphere and urban politics. Savage's account of weaving in Preston from the late nineteenth century to the interwar period illustrates the way in which patriarchal structures in the domestic sphere (the sphere of reproduction) extended to and were associated with patriarchy in the workplace. His evidence shows that in prewar Preston's weaving sheds it was unusual for (male) heads of households whose daughters or wives were employed as weavers to agree variations in working conditions (such as time off) directly with their (male) overseer, who – in the weaving shed – acted as a kind of surrogate head of household, regulating morals as well as quality of work. However, in the early twentieth century, though patriarchal relations remained, the role of the overseer in sustaining them was undermined by changes in both the forms of ownership of mills (joint stock companies with specialist managers becoming more usual), and state-sponsored change in the labour market – namely the introduction of National Insurance – which reduced the scope for discretion in recruitment on which overseer power rested in large measure. The case study demonstrates some of the links between the spheres of production and reproduction, and also, as Savage remarks, the intertwining of local conditions, changes in the management of capitalist enterprise and state policies implemented uniformly throughout the country.

Mark-Lawson and Warde (1987) explore the implications of gender relations in the workplace for urban politics, comparing Preston with the neighbouring towns of Lancaster and Nelson. The comparisons between Preston and Nelson, both cotton towns, are especially interesting. They are persuasive in arguing that the general segregation in Preston's labour market (whereby, weaving was largely a female occupation supervised by men, with men also employed in other industries to which women were not recruited) is central to understanding the low priority attached by the local Labour Party to welfare issues. The Preston Labour Party's links to trade unions, from which women were excluded by patriarchal attitudes and power, isolated women from it and also insulated the party from the influence of women activists. In Nelson, on the other hand, employment opportunities were not restricted to cotton, with the result that substantial numbers of men worked alongside women as weavers, both subject to the supervision of (male) overseers and managers. This experience of equality of conditions and lack of segregation in the labour market underpinned women's involvement in both trade unions and labour politics, with a correspondingly greater prominence attached to welfare issues than in Preston. Little (1999) has explored the implications of these kinds of spatial variations for the struggle for greater gender equality in planning, and they also help us understand the great differences in the willingness of local planning authorities to promote race equality (see Chapter 4), for we would expect the racialisation of social relations to exhibit some spatial variation, while still structured by an extra-local pattern of racialised power relations.

So, as Jeffers *et al.* (1996) note, the local differences in social relations are of considerably more than simply academic interest. One dimension of distinctively local racialisation of social relations is the ways in which images of place are created and projected.

Glenn Jordan (1988: 56), writing of Butetown in Cardiff, a multi-ethnic dockland area for over a century, commented that there have, historically, been: 'two...hegemonic narratives about Tiger Bay: a story about the area as dirty, sexually permissive and offensive and a story about the area as romantic, exotic and alluring'. These narratives have not been innocent descriptions, nor naïve misrepresentations. Rather, they have provided part of the political justification for the continuing stigmatisation of Butetown and its residents, and, in particular, a general lack of concern about the area's continuing poverty and the persistence of racial discrimination in the local labour market (Commission for Racial Equality 1991). When in the 1980s and 1990s governmental and private sector interest grew in the prospects of profitable development in Cardiff's docklands, a careful attempt had to be made by those selling the area to investors and tourists to reconstruct its image. So, for example, far from naming new developments or public houses to honour local heroes or the local vernacular, a not uncommon way of signifying local identity (Taylor *et al.* 1996: 29), new developments have names which have no local historical or cultural reso-nance but which convey signals to an audience outside the area. Thus one of the earliest 1980s developments has been called 'Atlantic Wharf', and a new public house is 'The Wharf'. Neither name has any local significance other than underlining in a non-specific way the maritime connections of the area which, in the late 1980s, were regarded as a marketing 'plus' (Thomas and Imrie 1993). Not surprisingly, the existing residents of Butetown have reser-vations about this process: an end to a stigmatisation of a place is a good thing as long as it extends to them as individuals and groups of people. However, the manner in which the area's planning has been conducted has not reassured them. As early as the mid-1980s, two activists in local commu-nity groups were complaining (with good reason) that: 'There seems to be a massive plan for the area that the community knew nothing about the past few weeks and whatever we try to do or say is considered a nuisance to that plan' (quoted in Anon. 1984).

They seem to be written out of the new planning narrative for what is now called 'Cardiff Bay' as effectively as they and their history are excluded from the new images of 'The Bay'. By the mid-1990s, it is difficult to read the emerging highway network – in particular, the excellent access roads from outside Butetown into the commercial/tourist waterfront strip – as anything other than ways of transporting investors, tourists and 'outsiders' in general, into the glitzy new attractions while bypassing the run-down municipal housing areas of Butetown. Residents have been granted no input into the alignment or status of new roads; their involvement had been limited to discussions of incidental open space alongside new highways

(Thomas 1995). In this example, some highway planning decisions and even the nomenclature of developments can be best understood within the context of the distinctive racialisation of social relations in Cardiff and its immediate hinterland. And far from challenging these processes, the planned redevelopment consolidates them, which shows the importance of a systematic analysis of the planning system and how that may be racialised.

Policy processes in planning

The purpose of this section is to consider how best to analyse planning systematically. The argument will be made that thinking of the planning system as a group of intertwined policy processes is a helpful first step. At one time I had the intention of using a typology of policy processes as a way of organising the whole book, but I now recognise the limitations of such an approach. Nevertheless, like others (Healey 1990; Stephenson 1998). I acknowledge the value of the notion of policy processes in understanding how planning works. In this section, having defined the idea, I give some illustrations of how policy processes in planning might be racialised.

Public policy making can be theorised as a (sometimes complex) interaction of policy processes, each defined in terms of access criteria and discourse criteria (Healey 1990). A strength of the policy process framework is that it provides a way of disentangling the complex mix of vocabularies, judgements and arenas (such as technical, political and legal) which can be conducted in parallel or sequentially during public policy making. The framework also lays bare the ways in which exclusion from different kinds of discussion of policy are legitimised and the ways in which credentials for one (such as discussions in a political forum) may be worthless in another (such as discussions between technical officers conducting a supposedly 'objective' and 'rational' appraisal of policy). However, the use of policy processes as an analytical device should not be taken to imply an acceptance of the criteria (or justifications) which define them: simply by recognising that, say, professional officers in local government manage to construct and restrict access to a (sometimes influential) arena for discussion and decision making by invoking notions of technical competence, rationality and objectivity, we (as analysts) do not endorse the notions of rationality and objectivity they use; nor are policy processes (and their interactions) static. Furthermore, delineating the type and scope of policy processes operating in a particular organisation, or policy area, does not of itself establish the distribution of power and influence within that organisation or policy area. The discussion of policy processes needs to be supplemented by an account of how the resources needed in order to gain entry to, and succeed in, the various processes are distributed. At an aggregate level, some of this data is available: we know, for example, that access to professional employment is ethnically skewed (Jones 1993; Nadin and Jones 1990), save, perhaps, for the small area of the 'equal opportunities community' (Cain and Yuval-Davis 1990). It has been argued before the Macpherson inquiry (1999a: 25), that an ethnically skewed workforce is more likely to generate and sustain a racist occupational culture. Where policy making is dominated by professionals, therefore, we would expect, all else being equal, that black and ethnic minority influence would be marginalised. Indeed, in many urban renewal projects areas there will be disproportionately few local residents (of any ethnic or racialised group) who would be granted a hearing in technical policy processes. The identification and disentangling of policy processes within policy making is intended, then, to make the vital first step in establishing the kinds of resources or strategies which are needed to gain influence over policy. A final limitation of too exclusive a focus on policy processes is that the origins of the criteria and values which define the process (discussed later) lie outside the process, in society at large, and can only be understood as such; otherwise they can only be construed as entirely arbitrary. This qualification is especially important if we wish to investigate the racialisation of a policy process, for in essence that involves examining the way in which the policy process uses and itself helps define racial categories which have a wider societal reach.

Healey (1990) identifies five processes which have been significant in public administration in Britain in the 1980s, and, especially in understanding planning over that period; Thomas *et al.* (1998) have suggested that one other has become important in the more fluid system of local governance in the 1990s (see Table 2.1). Typically, more than one process is involved in any given policy making episode, and Healey points out that just as the significance of each may vary from time to time and place to place, so might its detailed specification (that is, the answers to the questions set out in Table 2.3).

The establishment of the criteria featured in Table 2.3 is a social process, which can be racialised (and will be contested). For example, Solomos and Back (1995: chs 4–5) discuss the criteria governing involvement in party politics in Birmingham in the 1980s and 1990s. They note diverse ways in which Labour politics in the city was racialised, one of which was the assumption among powerful white politicians that a quasi-corrupt 'patronage politics' was somehow natural in the Indian sub-continent (1995: 99). Many white Labour activists were willing to be complicit with this kind of politics, even if disagreeing with it in principle, because they saw it as 'natural'. One consequence was that one of the major routes for Asian access to Labour party politics was, indeed, mediated by influential patrons from within the 'community' (1995: ch. 4). This kind of arrangement may affect not only the proportion of racialised minorities involved in local politics, but also their gender. Thus Geddes (1993) found not only an under-representation of ethnic minorities among councillors, but also a gross under-representation of women among ethnic minority councillors.

Table 2.1 Policy processes in public administration in Britain in the 1980s

Bureaucratic-legal	the determination of actions in terms of formal procedural and legal rules.
Techno-rational	the determination of actions in terms of the judgement of experts and scientific reasoning.
Semi-judicial	the determination of actions through formal hearings of the arguments of conflicting interests, with an assessor balancing the relative merits of the arguments.
Consultative	the determination of actions through negotiation and debate with, and among, concerned and affected groups; the forms of such consultation may include privatism, or more purist forms.
Politico-rational	the determination of action by the judgement of politicians in the formal arenas of representative democracy.
Nominee	the determination of actions by the judgements of nominees of the state, operating as managers of agencies with no direct electoral accountability.

Sources: Healey et al. (1992: 224); Thomas et al. (1998).

These generalisations can mask spatial variations. The general message of Saggar's (1998) review of British politics is of racialised marginalisation, with Gifford (1998: vviii) claiming that, 'whenever two or more black politicians are gathered together, the talk is of the prejudice they suffered from within their own party, as well as outside'. Yet in the same book, Nanton (1998) finds some examples of well-connected ethnic minority community leaders, and Le Lohé (1998: 94) argues that 'it does now...seem that Asian people participate fully in British politics both as voters and as councillors', though with great variations across space and across different ethnic groups.

The techno-rational policy process provides an example of possible indirect racialisation. Here, the under-representation of racialised minorities in the planning profession (Nadin and Jones (1990), give a figure of 3 per cent of the profession's being black and ethnic minorities) will limit their involvement in a policy process where certain professional credentials are necessary

Table 2.2 Illustrations of policy processes in British planning

Bureaucratic-legal	application of development plan policies in development control.
Techno-rational	discussions between planning officers, highway officers and other technical officers on, for example, safety issues.
Semi-judicial	public inquiries, for example, into local plans or planning appeals
Consultative	public meetings, exhibitions and so on designed to elicit public comment; discussions between local plans.
Politico-rational	discussions of planning policy, or key decisions, in party group meetings.
Nominee	discussion of higher management tiers of urban development corporations.

Sources: Healey et al. (1988: 224); Thomas et al. (1998).

to gain standing. (Of course, under-representation in planning has to be set against the position in other relevant professions, such as surveying and architecture, where the position may be healthier; see de Graft-Johnson 1999: 21). No convincing explanation has been offered as to why the planning profession does not recruit more entrants from black and ethnic minorities, but the possibility of racialised criteria playing a part, perhaps subtly, at key entry points (career advice in school, university entrance and so on) cannot be discounted, although recent study found no evidence of this (Liverpool John Moores University 1998). The same study did find fewer references to equal opportunities in recruitment advertisements by private sector planning organisations than by those in the public sector, with both well behind housing organisations (Liverpool John Moores University 1998: 30). Jenkins (1986) has drawn attention to the distinction between *suitability criteria* for employment (skills, qualification, experience) and *acceptability criteria* (in essence, how will the candidate fit in). The latter – which, typically, are not set out publicly – can be especially significant in recruiting for teams (such as in planning offices) and are often racialised (Carter 1999). Whether racialised entry criteria for employment or promotion are unwittingly employed in public (and especially) private sector planning organisations merits further investigation.

Table 2.3 The defining criteria of policy processes in public administration

---

1 *Criteria governing who is involved:*
   who gets access to the process and on what terms
   who controls the process
   to whom must the process be legitimated

2 *Criteria governing the relations between those involved:*
   what style of debate
   what procedure of debate

3 *Criteria governing the judgement of an acceptable decision:*
   which values should govern the decision
   in what way should decisions be presented to the relevant constituency

---

Source: Healey et al. (1988: 223).

The *values* governing the acceptability of decisions might also be determined in a racialised process. We have noted, for example, how an implicitly racialised conception of what constitutes appropriate behaviour and social relations in a rural English village can be introduced into discussions of planning applications. Interestingly, the application for the use of Bhaktivedanta Manor for public worship was granted by the Secretary of State on appeal, having not been determined by the local planning authority, which had a history enforcement action against such use. This is heartening evidence that shifts in values are possible; but it would be naïve to overlook the evidence that conservative interpretations of the public interest influence decision making in semi-judicial policy processes, and are even more significant in the formal judicial process (Blackman 1991; McAuslan 1980; Griffith 1997). So, for example, the idea that the public interest involves the retention of 'residential amenity' (peace and quiet and segregation of uses – in effect, a particular way of life) can be a powerful barrier to the development of community facilities (or commercial enterprises) by racialised minorities in inner areas (Farnsworth 1989; Thomas 1994b). As for criteria governing relations between participants in policy processes, the persuasiveness of racialised stereotypes can affect initial judgements of whether particular racialised minorities are capable of, or are actually adhering to, the norms which help define particular policy processes.

In the racialisation of policy processes, the precise character of a process and racial categories are defined jointly, just as was discussed earlier in relation to space and race. And, as with space, these definitions are fluid rather than fixed: they are reaffirmed or modified in daily interactions, particularly (but not exclusively) in explicit struggles to change their nature. Finally, the precise nature of policy processes will vary over space, as do social relations.

Duncan and Goodwin (1988: 114) argue that local state institutions are rooted in the heterogeneity of local social relations, where central states have difficulty in dealing with this differentiation. Local states assist central government in dealing with spatial variation, but can also act as the voice of local resistance. The precise way in which public policy is racialised in a particular locality will thus be an historically contingent product of interaction between specifically local and extra-local factors. A book such as this can therefore offer only a broad overview and, it is hoped, a framework for analysis and action.

Chapter 3 will outline the changing nature of the racialisation of British society and public policy in the post-1945 period. At times, planning contributed to the form racialisation took, if only to reaffirm trends which had a greater impetus from developments in other fields of public policy; however, as we shall see, it was mainly outside planning – for example, in relation to immigration policy, housing and urban policy – that some of the most influential struggles and debates over racial ideologies took place.

Notes

1 This section draws heavily on Thomas et al. (1995).
2 Appadurai (1999) argues convincingly that the racialisation of ethnicity can mean that markers of ethnicity are useless, and then invisible (indeed, fictive) markers are employed: this, he claims, is one of the perverted rationales of the horrific (but systematic) injuries inflicted on victims of self-styled inter-ethnic conflict.

   A less dramatic example of the use of non-obvious markers (or, at least, non-definable markers) of ethnicity relates to the criteria used by the Office of Population Census and Surveys (OPCS) in counting gypsies:

   > the definition of who should be counted would include certain non-nomadic gypsies and be based on the concept of a 'gypsy identity'. OPCS does not consider it necessary to define a 'Gypsy' since, in practice, counting staff appear to have little difficulty in defining them.
   >
   > (Green 1991: 7)

3 See for example, the BBC television documentary 'The Road to Hare Krishna', broadcast in the *Everyman* series on BBC1, 2 October 1994. The planning history and arguments can be found in the inspector's report, and the ministerial decision letter for the relevant planning application is DETR reference no. APP/N1920/A/94/241083.
4 Though the discussion which follows is couched in terms of 'occupational cultures', it could be presented in terms of 'organisational cultures', ways in which understandings of the social would grow up within an organisation as a basis for action and policy.

Chapter 3

Race, public policy and planning in postwar Britain

Introduction

Popular xenophobia and the encouragement, and exploitation, of racism are central themes in twentieth-century world history, including that of Britain (Hobsbawm 1994). However, it is from the 1950s that Britain's politics has been overtly racialised, a process which has continued until the present. This postwar period is also one which has seen a transformation of the scale and nature of town and country planning in Britain (Ward 1994; Cullingworth 1999). One of the arguments in this book is that we can better understand postwar British planning if we locate it against the background of the racial-isation of public policy making. Planning was not one of the policy areas at the centre of the new form of racialised politics, but neither was it unaffected. The chapter begins by sketching aspects of the racialisation of three public policy areas: immigration, housing and urban policy. There were (and are) other important terrains for struggle – notably, employment, education and health – and giving anything less than a full picture is difficult to justify intellectually. The justification is partly pragmatic; there is a need to press on to look at the planning system. In addition, excellent reviews exist of these other topics (for example Mason 1995; Solomos 1993), and those chosen for discussion in this chapter have a particular relevance to planning, and provide important lessons for those interested in analysing planning in a racialised society. The second part of the chapter will focus on planning in particular, considering the extent to which its origins and postwar history have inhibited serious engagement with issues of race equality.

Immigration, housing and urban policy, and the control of immigration have been at the heart of what Solomos (1993) has characterised as an increasingly overtly racialised politics in postwar Britain. When Smith (1989) argues that the racialisation of political discussion occurred in three phases, with breaks in 1958–62 and 1979, immigration controls are key indicators of the changes she wishes to highlight. It is, of course, non-white immigra-tion to which we are referring here. Irish immigration is a well-established phenomenon. Chance (1996) estimates that in 1991 there were over 800,000

Irish born residents in Great Britain, the overwhelming majority of whom were white; bearing in mind that 150 years of substantial immigration has created an even larger pool of people of Irish descent, it is clear that Irish immigration is a substantial component of Britain's ethnic mix. Though the postwar politics of immigration revolves around regulating the flow of non-white immigrants, this is not to deny that there is also a long and inglorious history of anti-Irish racism in Britain (see for example O'Leary 1991). Indeed, Hickman and Walter (1997) argue that the extent of contemporary racism directed against Irish people has been obscured by the politicisation of non-white immigration.

The demographic context for the discussion which follows was outlined in Chapter 1. The figures presented there make clear the way in which the origins of immigrants changed in the postwar period from a period of Caribbean dominance in the 1950s and 1960s to one of Asian dominance from the mid-1960s. In addition, the type of immigrant changed over time, with the proportion of economically active males falling from the 1970s and the proportion of dependants growing (Brown 1984). These changes were heavily influenced by labour market conditions in Britain, and also a racialised politics of immigration in the UK, resulting in particular in the progressive tightening of legislation controlling immigration.

The key postwar legislation is set out in Table 3.1, and there are a number of good accounts of the significance of successive enactments (Solomos 1993). For our purposes, we need to highlight what the clear trend in legisla-tion *represented*, and what it said about British political and public life.

First, and perhaps most importantly of all, the evident racism of the legislation – its increasingly explicit targeting of non-white ethnic minorities – was possible because of an increasingly overt racialisation of British poli-tics in general (Solomos 1993). Racism has long been a part of British politics, and there have been sporadic attempts in the early twentieth century to control the influx of 'aliens', typically as a sop to defuse social tensions in Britain (Mason 1995). But in the 1950s, for example, government attempts to regulate black immigration were covert (Solomos 1993); it was not politi-cally acceptable to operate openly a racially based immigration system. Yet though resolutions calling for immigration controls – such as that of inner London Labour parties in the 1950s, documented by Goss (1988) – could be sidelined or smothered at party conferences, there was no fundamental attack on racialised political analyses themselves. So, while political leaders might disfavour and disapprove of racism and racist violence, they appeared to accept it as a 'natural' response to certain kinds of (perhaps extreme) circumstances: to act as if one were a member of a racial group and to have an antipathy towards other racial groups was unfortunate, perhaps reprehen-sible but, as it were, a fact of life.

This view underpinned the concern of political leaders to limit immigration,

Table 3.1 Key legislation controlling immigration to Britain

1948	British Nationality Act: distinction drawn between citizens of United Kingdom (and its colonies), and Commonwealth citizens, but both having right to enter, settle and work in Britain.
1962	Commonwealth Immigrants Act: all holders of Commonwealth passports subject to immigration control, except those who were (a) born in Britain; (b) held British passports issued by the British government; or (c) persons included in the passport of someone falling under (a) or (b). Other Commonwealth citizens required a voucher to enter Britain.
1968	Commonwealth Immigrants Act: any citizen of Britain or its colonies who held a passport issued by the British government would be subject to immigration control unless they or at least one parent or grandparent was born, adopted, naturalised or registered in Britain as a citizen of Britain or its colonies. [political context: seeking to control immigration by East African Asians].
1971	Immigration Act: all aliens and Commonwealth citizens who were not patrials needed permission to enter Britain. Non-patrials entered with work-permits, and had no right of settlement. Among those defined as patrials, were:
	• citizens of Britain and its colonies who had citizenship by birth, adoption, naturalisation or registration in Britain, or who were born of parents one of whom had British citizenship by birth, or one of whose grandparents had such citizenship;
	• citizens of Britain and its colonies who had citizenship by birth, adoption, naturalisation or registration in Britain, or who were born of parents one of whom had British citizenship by birth, or one of whose grandparents had such citizenship; citizens of Britain and its colonies who had at any time settled in Britain and who had been ordinarily resident in Britain for five years or more.
1981	British Nationality Act: created three kinds of citizenship: British citizens; British Dependent Territories citizens; British overseas citizens. Only first had automatic right to abode in Britain (in 1983 and 1990 Acts were passed to make provision for Falkland Islanders and a limited number of Hong Kong residents, respectively, to acquire citizenship).

Source: mainly based on Solomos (1993).

and thereby the 'provocation' to racial tension, while simultaneously outlawing the worst manifestations of racial discrimination. While maverick politicians might introduce racism into party politics, such as happened at the Smethwick by-election of 1964 (Solomos 1993), the major national political parties established what Saggar (1991) has referred to as a 'liberal settlement' which would marginalise it as a party political issue. The core of this settlement was the acceptance of ever stricter controls on immigration coupled with government support for measures to promote racial harmony, through integration.

Two quotations from prominent politicians of the 1960s, quoted by Smith (1989: 123–4) give a flavour of the argument:

> the greater the numbers coming into the country the larger will these communities become and the more difficult it will be to integrate them into our national life...
>
> (Tory minister 'Rab' Butler)

> without integration, limitation is inexcusable; without limitation, integration is impossible.
>
> (Labour minister Roy Hattersley)

However, while the control of immigration was pursued with some vigour, there were less successful attempts at putting in place mechanisms for promoting racial harmony (to be supplemented by a concern for equality only late in the 1960s). From 1965 a series of Race Relations Acts (the last passed in 1976) formally outlawed discrimination based on 'colour, race, nationality, or ethnic or national origin' in whole areas of public life. The *primary* focus of the Acts, however, and of the agencies set up to promote their implementation, was that discrimination be eradicated from the provision of housing, and in employment and education. Spatial issues, which might have brought planning more into the centre of discussions about equality of opportunity, have not been a major concern. Thus there has been no addressing of the question of breaking down the historic residential segregation which has characterised British cities. Smith has argued persuasively that this lack of concern for spatial distribution of the population betrayed the deep-rooted racialisation of white popular and political opinion; as the Butler quote above hints, with its reference to 'communities' there was a view that there was something 'natural' about 'people of the same kind' (that is, a 'race') living together. Such views helped sustain a conception of Englishness which viewed black immigration as a territorial threat. Smith (1989: 120) tellingly quotes Enoch Powell's reference in 1968 to English people finding 'their homes and neighbourhoods changed beyond recognition' and 'the transformation of whole areas...into alien territory'. If Powell were a political maverick, he nevertheless enjoyed considerable popular appeal and articulated many ideas which were held more generally. In addition, Powell's ideas of 'race' and other matters were precursors of the New Right agenda of the late 1970s, and subsequently Margaret Thatcher's comments in 1979 were clear reiterations of his themes:

> Some people have felt swamped by immigrants. They've seen the whole character of their neighbourhood change…Of course people can feel that they are being swamped. Small minorities can be absorbed – they can be assets to the majority community – but once a minority in a neighbourhood gets very large, people do feel swamped. They feel their whole way of life has been changed.
>
> (*The Observer*, 25 February 1979, quoted by Solomos 1989: 83)

Thatcher's rhetoric is characteristically crude, and the apparent underlying acceptance of a vigorous popular reaction to immigration would not find favour with more liberal politicians, but the racialised analysis is no different from Hattersley's and Butler's. It is in this way that the politics of immigration has set the tone for popular perceptions and understandings of what it means for Britain to be a multi-ethnic or multi-racial society. Meanwhile, in a variety of other policy areas, there have been political and professional struggles to counter racism; housing is one of the more significant of these for planners, first because access to housing has implications for the spatial distribution of the population and second, because many of the debates in the housing field revolved around the role of public sector bureaucracies in the allocation of scarce resources, a task which planning authorities also undertake (Eversley 1973).

Housing

Adequate housing and a reasonable income are two key elements of anyone's quality of life. Moreover, in a society such as Britain's these elements are linked, though the complexities of these links, and especially their localised variations, are neither well studied nor understood (Moore 1992). The manner in which racism and more indirect racial discrimination have operated to limit access to housing has been the object of some of the best-known postwar research on racialised inequality in British society, mostly conducted in the period up to the late 1980s (Karn and Phillips 1998). In relation to public sector (or 'social') housing, Phillips (1987: 213) summarised the general picture presented in a series of studies of complex processes: 'All present a similar picture: black people tend to wait longer for housing, are more likely to be allocated poorer property and more frequently end up on less desirable estates.'

A more recent review was slightly more optimistic, drawing attention to the increased acceptance by 'social landlords' of the need to guard against racism in housing allocation, emphasising the success of Black and Ethnic Minority Housing Associations (though some face an uncertain future) and recognising that, in general, access to social housing was easier that it had been in earlier decades. Nevertheless, while the authors accept that real gains have been made in combating institutional and direct discrimination they feel:

> that it is not coincidental that improved access for ethnic minorities to social rented housing has come at a time when the sector has lost status and desirability, becoming a 'residual tenure' for 'residual groups'.
>
> (Karn and Phillips 1998: 138)

These outcomes suggest that forms of institutionalised discrimination remain in operation; that is, that certain kinds of procedures and bureaucratic rules and judgements are bearing disproportionately heavily on black and ethnic minorities. However, difficulties in the social rented sector force ethnic minorities to rely the more heavily on private sector housing, either for rent or owner occupation. However, here too they have encountered institutional barriers (such as unwillingness on the part of building societies to lend money) and direct racism (vendors or estate agents unwilling to sell). As long ago as 1967, Rex and Moore's landmark analysis of the dynamics of residential segregation in Sparkbrook, in inner Birmingham, identified these issues. It contained important lessons which planners had barely absorbed even twenty years later (Krishnarayan and Thomas 1993). The Sparkbrook study demonstrated how bureaucratic procedures which were just and fair in formal terms (inasmuch as they were applied equally to everyone) could have systematically different outcomes according to one's race or ethnicity. In the Birmingham case, public sector housing was allocated to people registered on a waiting list, to be on which one had to have worked or lived in the city for five years, a requirement which bore disproportionately heavily on the (predominantly non-white) immigrants to the city. In addition, some of the circumstances which qualified for housing 'points' (which had to be accumulated to qualify for housing) – such as war service or length of time on the waiting list – would also tend to put immigrants at a disadvantage. Even in the 1980s and 1990s, many professional planners find it difficult to accept that bureaucratic systems such as development control or other aspects of planning can systematically cause disproportionate problems for certain sectors of the population, even when there is not necessarily any intention to do so. Rex and Moore also emphasised the significance of professional judgement and discretion – in their case, the judgement of Housing Visitors of the domestic standards of would-be tenants – in sometimes unwittingly discriminating against people whose culture or values might be unfamiliar. Again, this is a lesson which was not publicly acknowledged by British planners until the late 1970s, as will be discussed later in this chapter.

Excluded from public sector housing, immigrants would also find themselves failing to meet requirements for building societies for loans. In addition, they were the victims of crude racism. The result was their borrowing money from other sources to buy cheap large houses, often in poor repair, which could be sub-let to help pay for the loans used to buy them. Rex and Moore documented and analysed the creation of residential areas which were distinctive both physically and socially. Because the black population held a distinctive and precarious economic position and because their demographic structure was distinctive (particularly, at that time, the immigrants from the Indian sub-continent, who were predominantly male), their housing needs and general use of space tended to be distinctive also. Residential segregation emphasised this, creating large areas with particular characteristics and specialised planning concerns. Decades were to pass, however, before some local planning authorities recognised the value of drawing up policies which catered for the spatially concentrated needs of black and ethnic minorities, for example in identifying appropriate sites or areas for new places of worship. This lack of sensitivity, it has been argued, has been a product of the imperviousness of both political and professional decision making in planning to the influence of black and ethnic minorities (Thomas and Krishnarayan 1994).

Studies such as those of Rex and Moore have been landmarks in developing an understanding of racialised social processes, and we can still benefit from familiarity with them. However, much has changed – in the economy, in governance and in social mores and the law – in the last few decades, and a number of recent reviews have emphasised the diversity of experiences and fortunes of different ethnic groups in housing, employment, education and other aspects of life (Karn and Phillips 1998; Modood *et al.* 1997; Peach 1996d). In relation to housing, Karn and Phillips (1998: 152) contend that 'ethnic minority disadvantages have persisted into the 1990s' as a result of direct and indirect discrimination, but they also emphasise the need for research to improve our understanding of the complex processes which give rise to the outcomes covered by such a generalisation. This is a key message for public policy as a whole (including planning): resources must be devoted consistently to understanding the context within which policy is being implemented and to understanding the effects of policy.

Beyond that, the analyses and reviews of housing policy have six key lessons for planning practice. Three of these are elaborated by Phillips (1987: 227–33) in her discussion of the difficulties faced by anti-racism strategies in housing. She identifies three key issues, from each of which planners have much to learn, as follows.

(1) Bureaucratic processes can encourage, *by creating a demand for*, discriminatory practices. Phillips's example is the use of negative stereotypes

of black people in housing allocation; these stereotypes influenced the discretionary judgements of housing officers at certain important stages in the allocation process. Clearly, it is important to shake the grip of these stereotypes on the minds of individual officers; but, Phillips points out, it is also vital to understand the ways which stereotypes may be operationally useful, might help individuals manage their workload, and the need to address *that* issue, so that the *need* for stereotyping can be reduced. The same point can be made about any bureaucratic process, including planning, and later in this chapter the significance of bureaucratisation of planning is explored.

(2) In working to eradicate discrimination, we need to bear in mind both the influence of social structure and individual agency. Consider Rex and Moore's analysis, for example. They point out the significance of procedures and rules ('structural' factors, in the sense of not being at the behest of particular individuals), but they also note the role of discretionary judgements by individuals (such as housing visitors). It is important to modify structural factors leading to discrimination, but we must not overlook the areas within which discretionary judgements by individuals can be exercised, and the pressures on these individuals/or the material interests wrapped up in their judgements) which may push them towards discriminatory action. Phillips's example is of a housing estate manager whose personal interests might be best served by sustaining segregation if he or she believes that might reduce racist violence; in seeking a 'quiet life', he or she might be willing to reduce choice within the housing stock for all ethnic or racial groups. Planners too have wide areas of discretion, and the exercise of this discretion needs to be scrutinised: for example, local planning authorities are notoriously conservative in dealing with planning applications for hot food takeaways, as they strive to pacify local residents who invariably object to the applications. It is arguable that the consequences of this conservative use of their discretion bear disproportionately harshly on those black and ethnic minority groups who rely heavily on the take away sector for employment (Thomas 1994b).

(3) Phillips has a third point which is also very pertinent for planners. She points out that housing allocations (or, for that matter, the planning system) do not exist in social or institutional isolation. Disadvantage in one sphere can inhibit the ability to take advantage of opportunities in another. Her example relates to housing – a fair system of allocation may offer all potential tenants a wide range of housing, but the potential tenants may not be able to take advantage of this choice if they are tied to particular types of employment (perhaps because of discrimination in the labour market). Planners too need to be aware of the socio-economic context within which they are acting; no one – whether a member of an ethnic minority or not – enters the planning system without any kind of social or economic background. Inevitably, people bring this background and context to the planning system, and in turn, the outcomes of the planning system will be

interpreted (and judged) in terms of how they impact on individuals lives as a whole. Thus some planning authorities have recognised the importance of certain kinds of business in providing employment for black and ethnic minorities whose prospects of employment in other sectors can be disproportionately poor (Krishnarayan and Thomas 1993). They have taken this fact into account in devising their local plan policies; it does not trump all other considerations, but it is an important considerations alongside others in the shaping of policy.

To these, we might add three further lessons:

(4) The struggle to promote race equality is not won simply by introducing new procedures or regulations, important as these may be. Karn and Phillips point out the continuing gap between the ethnic monitoring of certain housing procedures, and policy development. Yet, there can be little doubt that the Commission for Racial Equality's investigation and codes of practice in housing (CRE 1984) have played an important part in improving the sensitivity of those involved in providing public and private sector housing to the possibility of racial discrimination.

(5) The racialised ethnic residential segregation which is so characteristic of larger British towns and cities is the product of social processes. It is not 'natural' or inevitable (indeed, there is evidence of a dispersal of some ethnic groups between 1981 and 1991 (Peach 1996c)). Moreover, such segregation is a product of a mix of factors, which will operate to varying degrees at any one time, and in any particular place. Foremost still are a variety of structural constraints which limit choice, including bureaucratic roles and procedures, and also the knock-on effects of disadvantages in the labour market (Karn and Phillips 1998). However, it is clear too that segregation can be a choice for minority ethnic residents who have few financial constraints; such choices are themselves complicated, of course, and may be outcomes of racial ideologies or reactions to racism (or fears of it), or reflect a value placed on the provision of certain cultural facilities (Peach 1996). It is almost inevitable that planners, the focus of whose work is the way towns and cities work and the patterns they form, will develop very clear views of how the city fits together. Such views are probably important in facilitating day to day activity, but planners must remember that these patterns are dynamic products of social processes, including racialised processes. The patterns cannot be ignored, but need not be endorsed; and they can be changed, and are changing (see for example Watt (1998) on generational differences in the creation and use of racialised spaces).

(6) Finally, the story of struggle for racial equality in housing reminds us of the importance of allowances between those most directly affected by discrimination and policy makers wishing to promote change. Black and ethnic minority housing associations, for example, are organisations founded within minority communities which are widely judged to have provided a valuable housing service to the whole community (a number have a substan-

tial proportion of white tenants) (Franklin and Passmore 1998; Harrison *et al.* 1996).

Urban policy

'Urban policy' is a term of art, and with the majority of the area of towns and cities devoted to housing it is arguable that housing policy, traditionally analysed and discussed separately, should be regarded as a key component of it. However, over the last thirty years or so the term has been used for a loose collection of policies aimed at addressing or mitigating the effects of a series of apparently distinctively urban problems (Atkinson and Moon 1994). Many, especially in recent years, have had an economic focus, but environmental, educational and law and order concerns have featured from time to time. The policies have been discussed and evaluated at some length elsewhere (Atkinson and Moon 1994; Robson *et al.* 1994), though there is surprisingly little hard evidence of their effects on racialised minorities. Of more interest to us in this chapter is the way that in postwar Britain the conceptualisations of the urban 'problems' which policies have been meant to address have been increasingly racialised.

In Britain, cities have evoked ambivalent responses among intellectuals, the public at large and politicians, since the enormous urbanisation associated with industrialisation (Raban 1974; Williams 1975). There is a long history of 'respectable' anxiety about urban unrest, urban squalor and, in a word, the 'otherness' of the urban poor (Morris 1994). There is also a history of eliding concern about the physical and social conditions of the city with a belief in the irredeemability of poor city dwellers. The postwar immigration by black and ethnic minorities introduced a new dimension to these anxieties. Solomos (1993) reviews how ethnic minority immigrants were associated in an increasingly racialised popular and party political discourse with disease, dirt and overcrowding, crime and immorality. The evident residential segregation in larger cities provided a platform for the identification of the inner city with black and ethnic minorities and their associated ills. The fact that residential segregation by ethnicity or race is considerably less extreme in Britain than the USA shows again that these processes of attaching meanings to places, seeing them as places 'for' ethnic minorities, as 'dangerous places' and so on, is not a case of the 'facts speaking for themselves'. Such meanings are socially constructed and sustained. This is a complex process, but one aspect of it which is of particular interest to planners is the role of the local press.

Smith (1985) and Thomas (1994c) have analysed the ways in which the local press present urban issues; Smith looked at the reporting of crime, and Thomas the reporting of urban renewal. Both recognise the influence of the local press in shaping local political agendas; for example, in the case of an area of Birmingham, Smith (1985: 240) comments on how the local evening paper portrayed it for over a decade as an 'angry suburb', 'a neighbourhood where "our new multi-racial society sprawls drunkenly with all its conflicts raw, all its squalor exposed"'. But both emphasise that the local press uses popular stereotypes in its reporting; as Thomas (1994c) points out, the press must be perceived as being in touch with its readership, and as a result there is a tendency to use popular stereotypes, motifs and symbols in its reporting. Smith's (1985: 252) analysis of local press coverage of crime showed that, 'the provincial press provides a framework based on established social and spatial stereotypes...'.

The local press structures and guides discussion and debate, therefore, but does not do so in radically new directions. This has important implications for local government, including planning. Planning issues (defined broadly) are a staple of the local press (Cox and Morgan 1973), and a local planning authority (or group of planners) exploring an approach to planning, or a particular project, which challenges popular stereotypes (including racialised stereotypes) will need to be aware of the conservatism of the press, and attempt to anticipate and defuse potential criticism or misunderstanding. In addition, planners must be aware of the popular racialised stereotypes and image of the city, especially the inner city. It is likely that at least some councillors may be influenced by such stereotypes and images; for their part, planners must be wary of appearing to condone or support racialised images.

Both Smith (1985) and Burgess (1985) provide examples of the kinds of messages the media convey, and which reflect popular stereotypes. Smith (1985: 252) summarises her analysis of local press coverage of crime in Birmingham:

> the mass media sustained an image of coloured ethnic minorities as separate from mainstream society, particularly when dealing with the inner city. By linking race with crime, the news further defines these groups as part of a problem contributing to the risks of inner city life...

Burgess (1985) analysed national press coverage of the inner city disturbances of 1981. She found a more complex picture than that suggested by Smith, with what she terms a 'myth' of the inner city – that is, a supposedly descriptive account laced with meaning and interpretation – built up of four components:

- a portrayal of the physical environment as (generally) decayed, derelict and sleazy; the environment stood as a partial explanation of the desperation of the inhabitants, and an indictment of public policy (particularly when public sector housing was discussed);
- a discussion of white working-class communities in the inner city, and, in particular, alleged household and cultural characteristics which make

them dysfunctional, with single parent families, large numbers of children, poor educational attainment, and so on;

- a portrayal of the black population (interpreted, for the most part as population of the inner city) as volatile, criminal, unemployed, alienated, beset by generational conflict and hostile to the police;
- an emphasis on the 'street' as a central aspect of inner city life, and of street life as dangerous, consisting of a variety of illegal and/or anti-social behaviour including drug trafficking, prostitution, vandalism and graffiti, gambling and petty theft (particularly 'mugging').

Some clear themes are identified in this subtle analysis: the inner city is construed as a site of both physical and social/moral decay; this infects the whole population, white as well as black, but racial distinctions are significant in understanding what is going on. Such a view of the inner city builds upon long-standing myths about poor people, and their quarters (Morris 1994), myths to which planners have not been immune. Thus Wilfred Burns, one of the leading British planners of the 1960s, commented on the break-up of inner city communities as part of urban renewal:

> this is a good thing when we are dealing with people who have no initiative or civic pride. The task, surely, is to break up such groupings even though the people seem to be satisfied with their miserable environment and seem to enjoy an extrovert social life in their own locality.
> (Burns 1963: 94–5; quoted in Ward 1994: 153)

Here we have a conception of urban renewal as imposing a kind of social hygiene on cities, and a linking of physical and social objectives which is reminiscent of the pioneers of housing standards of a century earlier. The disruptive effect of clearance has been recognised by ethnic minority communities, many of whom have mobilised to oppose wholesale clearance, but the lack of political leverage enjoyed by minority communities means that stories of successful opposition are rare (see for example Stoker and Brindley 1985), and those of frustration more common (Heywood and Naz 1990).

Research has shown that as disruptive and damaging as actual clearance and rehousing could be the blight caused by inclusion in a clearance or redevelopment programme, even though there might be no immediate prospect of compulsory acquisition. The blight could take many forms. One was the impossibility of receiving government grants, or loans from building societies or other reputable sources, for home improvements or for house purchase (making the properties very difficult to sell). Another common form was a high turnover of population, as those who could afford to leave (for example, by renting more expensive properties, or by accepting a loss on a house that was owned) did so, and a more transient population replaced them. By the late 1960s, physical redevelopment and housing clearance had a reduced role in urban policy, with general environmental upgrading (including, but going beyond, the refurbishment of older housing) becoming more significant. However, the focus of urban policy was itself broadening, with the so-called 'rediscovery of poverty' from the mid-1960s; see, for example, the classic text by Coates and Silburn (1970). In 1968 a Labour government launched a programme which was to be a key component of urban policy for more or less the next twenty years: the Urban Programme (UP), originally entitled 'Urban Aid'. The programme was to have major reorientations during its existence (see below), but certain elements remained constant, and it defined a political and professional consensus in respect of how urban policy should be conceived and delivered.

First, the resources targeted under the UP were small in scale compared with mainstream funding of education, social services, health and so on, and were intended to meet 'special needs'. The targeting was spatial – a list of eligible local authority areas was drawn up – and there was a consistent tension between this spatial targeting and the realisation that the 'special needs' being addressed extended beyond the target areas. Nevertheless, the area-based approach remains central to British urban policy, even after the demise of the UP.

Second, elected local authorities had pivotal roles in the UP. UP funds were channelled through local authorities, and central government and UP funding had to be supplemented by local authority funding (in the ratio of 3:1). In effect, then, eligible projects had to satisfy both central government and local government criteria. Most projects were actually sponsored and undertaken by local authorities themselves, though some were undertaken by voluntary and community organisations. The private sector was not involved.

Finally, 'the subliminal presence of race [was a] factor in structuring the development of programmes' (Atkinson and Moon 1994: 234). Assisting ethnic minorities became an explicit objective of the UP from 1974, but as was noted earlier, the notion of 'the urban', and especially of the 'inner city', had been constructed in a racialised fashion for decades earlier (Brownill et al. 1996; Solomos 1993). Urban policy, then, is affected by (and is part of) the wider politics of race, and its focus has often been muddied by tensions, between New Right hostility to positive action to assist ethnic minorities, and the long-standing ambivalence of centrist and leftist parties towards acknowledging the seriousness of racism. As a result, as Harrison (1989: 51) notes: 'Although race is on the agenda as an aspect of policy, it is...very much subordinate to the goals of general economic and environmental regeneration'.

These three elements structured urban policy throughout the 1970s. By the end of the decade they were supplemented by a further factor: the belief that the kinds of problems which urban policy was targeting were manifestations of structural changes in the economy. Hailed by some commentators as 'the first serious attempt by a government in the postwar era to understand the nature and causes of Britain's urban problems' (Atkinson and Moon 1994: 66), the 1977 government White Paper 'Policy for the Inner Cities' summed up an emerging political and academic consensus that economic restructuring, international in scale, was the root cause of the de-industrialisation, and the consequent unemployment, population decline, social malaise and physical decay, of certain parts of British cities. The government's response involved intensified spatial targeting of urban policy, an attempt to broaden the 'partners' involved in local policy formulation and delivery to include the private sector and voluntary groups, while retaining a key role for elected local authorities, and a shift from funding 'social' projects (play schemes for children, for example) to funding 'economic' schemes (workshops for new businesses might be a typical example). It is debatable whether the policy responses matched the diagnosis of the problem (Atkinson and Moon 1994), and overall urban policy in the late 1970s and into the early 1980s had a similar 'feel' to that of ten years earlier.

This could hardly be said of urban policy in the late 1980s. The UP has been gradually diminishing in importance over a number of years, and is due to expire. But more important than the demise of a particular programme was the new policy frame within which urban problems were being defined and addressed (Solesbury 1993). From the early 1980s onwards, successive Conservative governments promoted, with increasing insistence, a set of policies and initiatives which were informed by the following principles. First, the primary objective of urban policy should be to facilitate market-based solutions to urban problems. Second, in practice, this meant facilitating property development (certainly for most of the 1980s): this was the so-called 'property-led' approach (Healey *et al.* 1992). Third, scarce resources for urban policy implementation should be distributed by competition rather than by an index of need, as a way of encouraging better thought-out projects (Oatley 1998). Finally (but by no means least significantly), the role of elected local authorities in formulating and delivering urban policy should be drastically diminished, and in particular, private sector perspectives should be given a greater prominence. Achieving this latter task has involved a number of devices, perhaps the primary one being the setting up of large numbers of single-purpose, short-term organisations to deliver particular strands of urban policy; urban development corporations (UDCs), City Challenge teams and Single Regeneration Budget (SRB) projects, to name but a few. Elected local authorities are involved in some of these to varying extents, but they never have the centrality they had with the UP, while private sector organisations are also involved to a far greater extent.

The election of the Labour government is likely to mark an adjustment in policy rather than a radical break (an urban White Paper is anticipated which will clarify the government's approach). Labour is certainly committed to combating social exclusion, but its prescription seems to exclude re-distribution of wealth and income (Levitas 1998). Labour has also stated that elected local authorities will have a central role in governing their communities, but they are required to work in partnership with other agencies, and competition for funds and performance league tables will continue (Blair 1998). Moreover, until the publication of the Macpherson Report in 1999, it was difficult to spot any urgency in Labour's discussion of racism and race equality. The style and tone is undoubtedly different – here are politicians personally comfortable in a multi-ethnic society – but specific actions are lower profile. The Macpherson Report recommended changes to education, the race relations legislation and policing, and suggested that even broader changes in social attitudes were necessary. There is some evidence of a 'Macpherson effect' – government departments and agencies reviewing their own record on race equality – but there was a similar flurry after the Scarman Report in the early 1980s, and there followed a bleak decade for equal opportunities (Ball and Solomos 1990).

The twists and turns in urban policy until the mid-1990s have been exhaustively reviewed in the literature (for example Atkinson and Moon 1994; Hambleton and Thomas 1995) and in this chapter it will suffice simply to note their apparent implications for Britain's ethnic minority population. The first point to make is that assessing the implications is not easy, as very little evaluation of this dimension of urban policy has been undertaken, nor has data been collected with a view to monitoring the impact of policy on ethnic minorities (Harrison 1989; Brownill et al. 1997; Russell et al. 1996). A major government-funded evaluation of urban policy has virtually nothing to say about its effects on black and ethnic minorities (Robson et al. 1994), an omission which is consistent with the ambivalence of urban policy in relation to acknowledging ethnic diversity, let alone widespread and persistent racism, in British society. What little evidence is available suggests that ethnic minorities were (and are) more likely to benefit from urban policy if certain conditions are met: first, that policy explicitly addresses combating racism and racial disadvantage (Ollerearnshaw 1988; Munt 1994); second, that funding leans towards 'social' projects and revenue expenditure (such as salaries and running costs) (Munt 1994) rather than 'economic' projects of a capital nature (such as buildings) (Ball 1988; Harrison 1989); and third, that projects and local policy delivery are not in the hands of short-term, 'quick fix' agencies working to tight deadlines (Brownill et al. 1997). Few of these conditions have held for any length of time in any single place in Britain.

There is, however, a little indirect evidence that some ethnic minority groups were disproportionately affected by the uncertainty caused by the ambitious 1980s urban renewal projects described earlier. Gibson and Longstaff (1982), for example, note that in Birmingham, though the first wave of clearance areas tended not to have large proportions of ethnic minority residents, the adjoining areas, often designated for future action,

did. As Ratcliffe (1992) comments, such designations typically made it difficult to raise loans on property and to sell them. Ratcliffe's own research
relates to the 1980s, by which time urban renewal had come to mean grant-
aided improvement of housing and the environment more generally, and
many local authorities, such as Birmingham, had employed 'liaison officers'
to facilitate communication between themselves and ethnic minority
communities.

Ratcliffe's conclusion, however, is that the local authority had no serious
intention of engaging ethnic minorities in decision making over urban
renewal, and the liaison officers were viewed as mere conduits for information. Urban renewal was still conceived by council officers as an essentially
technical operation and the (generally non-technical) liaison officers were,
therefore, marginalised in decision-making processes. Ratcliffe's findings
report on the situation in the late 1980s, but subsequent work by
Krishnarayan and Thomas (1993) in relation to the planning system in
general, and Brownill *et al.* (1997) in relation to urban development corporations (UDCs), suggests that nothing of substance has changed. Though
these research projects do not focus directly on the material impacts of
urban renewal on ethnic minorities, their findings that ethnic minority voices
are marginal in the renewal process do not give any reason for optimism
about what those impacts might be.

More generally, the development of British urban policy illustrates the
insidious effects of the racialisation of public policy and politics in postwar
Britain. On the one hand, there appears to have been a clear shift towards
identifying the city as a locus of social problems and viewing the concentration of racialised minorities living there as part of the problem. On the other
hand, there has been reluctance to acknowledge the prevalence of racism
and to tackle it head on as part of urban policy (Munt 1994), a legacy of the
'liberal settlement' referred to earlier. Until this is done, the promotion of
race equality will always be a by-product of urban policy, either intended
but unacknowledged as too politically sensitive, (which contributes to racialisation), or accidental. Either way, this is an unsatisfactory approach to
creating a fairer society. Within planning, a more open approach is desirable.

This extremely selective review of some areas of public policy other than
planning has had two purposes. First, it has sought to explain the sources of
some of the racialised ideas and imagery – for example, about the changes in
Britain's cities and about the changing composition of its population –
which are likely to have affected planners as much as any other part of the
population. Second, in the case of housing policy, it has tried to identify
lessons for those promoting equal opportunities policies in planning, lessons
deriving from common features of planning and housing services.

The latter part of the chapter will discuss the racialisation of planning in
the postwar period, illustrating the ways in which broader concerns in public
policy have had an impact on it and also characteristics of its racialisation

which have been distinctive of it. To understand the postwar period, however, some (very selective) knowledge of British planning in the twentieth century is desirable.

Social policy, planning policy and race

This section will review the way in which the concerns of British town planning have become narrowed, and – in particular – divorced from social welfare issues over the course of the twentieth century. It is argued that this process helped inhibit (and continues to inhibit) attempts to think through the implications for planning of operating in a racialised society. For very many decades, a number of interests were served by reconstituting town planning as a supposedly technical activity related only distantly to social welfare. The nascent profession was dominated for some time by engineers, architects and surveyors; and, in any event, the claim to professionalism – especially dear to those with no other professional affiliations – was easier to defend if it revolved around a claim to *technical* expertise. For powerful commercial and industrial interests which advocated a modicum of planning, the activity was intended to involve only enough regulations to stop landowners obstructing the spatial restructuring associated with economic development: it was not a tool for radical social engineering. The judiciary, for its part, was ever conservative in its interpretation of the scope of planning legislation.

The process of defining planning as a technical built environment profession was well under way by the 1950s, and the popular and political identification of race as a 'social problem' of the first order from that period was no encouragement to planners to try to relate the significance of racism and racial disadvantage to their work. Nevertheless, the exposure of some planners to the day to day reality of life in a racialised society meant that during the 1970s a lobby developed within the professional institute which sought to put 'race and planning' on the professional agenda. In the later 1970s, this view was consistent with the increasing recognition (not always positive) of central and local government that urban policy had inter-related economic, social and environmental dimensions. In the 1980s and 1990s central government has emphasised a crudely functional relationship between land use planning and economic development, and has minimised the significance of social welfare or social justice for planning. The Royal Town Planning Institute, however, has persisted quite doggedly in promoting equal opportunities (including race equality) as an important professional concern.

This section adopts a broadly chronological approach in analysing the relationship between social welfare and town planning, as promoted (or played down) by both the professional institute and central and local government. It begins by considering, in a broad-brush fashion, planning from the early years of the twentieth century to the 1970s.

Social conservatism and town planning in Britain

One way of viewing the history of British planning up to the 1970s is to emphasise the narrowing of the scope and aspirations of the activity. Influential figures in the late nineteenth century and early twentieth century debates about the virtues of town planning conceived of the planning of land uses as part of a wider process of fashioning social change; some for essentially conservative ends (as in the company settlements of Saltaire and Port Sunlight with their concern for social control (Bell and Bell 1969)), others with more radical conceptions of social change, as implied in the original title of Howard's (1985) famous book, *Tomorrow: A Peaceful Path to Real Reform*. Although a portion of this early, holistic, often contradictory view of planning's potential has survived within pressure groups, notably the Town and Country Planning Association (TCPA) (Hardy 1991a; 1991b), the development of planning as an activity of the state has followed a different trajectory. As Ward (1994: 5) puts it, 'the state generally adopted town planning for reasons rather different to those which motivated the Town Planning movement to invent it'.

The weakness of a Whig view of the history of planning was referred to in Chapter 2. On the Whig view, state intervention in the property market and development process is seen as a 'natural' response to social and urban 'problems', so that the history of planning is seen as a tale of inevitable and progressive appreciation of and response to those problems (Hague 1984; Rees and Lambert 1985). Analyses of the earliest British planning legislation (McDougall 1979) and later developments (Hague 1984) have highlighted the way in which it emerged from processes of political struggle, a particular feature of which were attempts on the part of the non-land-owning classes to curb the economic (and ultimately political) power of landowners. Although such terminology might smack of a distinctively Marxist or neo-Marxist interpretation of British planning history, the general thrust of the argument is widely acknowledged. Thus McAuslan's (1980) detailed analysis of twentieth-century planning legislation in Britain, with its somewhat idealist conceptual framework of competing ideologies vying for supremacy within planning law, nevertheless identifies the degree to which private property rights (and especially landed property rights) are to be sustained (or overridden, or expropriated) as a key issue defining competing ideologies. In brief, then, town planning as a state activity was not introduced, and has not been maintained, in order to create some kind of egalitarian new society or to promote radical social reform. Against this background it is not surprising that, in practice, the administration of British planning has tended to focus on legal and technical aspects of land use and development and has not involved persistent and wide-ranging debates about the social purposes and goals of planning; although at certain moments – for example, the immediate post-1945 period – more radical prospects have been held out for a short time (Hardy 1991b).

This narrowing of focus has in general been congenial to and supported by the increasingly significant profession of town planners, as represented by the Royal Town Planning Institute (RTPI). Formed in 1914 as a qualifying association (that is, a putative professional organisation, entry to which was regulated by examination) the RTPI has become a major force in shaping the everyday practice of planning in the postwar period, as a specialised state bureaucracy has developed to administer the comprehensive planning system set up in 1947. The growth of the bureaucracy and its significance for the profession are noted by Cherry, a historian of the professional institute. Speaking of the 1950s, Cherry writes, 'The membership of the Institute as a whole was now very largely local authority staff' (1974: 162). And although not all state planners were members of the professional institute, the RTPI has gradually increased its influence among them. The proportion of planners who were members was 57 per cent in 1950, and had increased to 70 per cent in 1963–4 (Faludi 1978: 44). Today, membership of the RTPI is widely regarded as an essential qualification for public sector planners.

The RTPI was founded jointly by the existing professional organisations representing architects, engineers and surveyors and, though it has widened the intellectual basis of its membership in the last eighty years, the concern with the physical technicalities of land development has remained a major preoccupation of the RTPI and its membership. Doubtless this has in part reflected the predilections of members, but it has also been reinforced by the nature of the planning system its members were being required to work within (see below). Moreover, as Healey and Underwood (1978) have documented in relation to London boroughs, interdepartmental and interprofessional rivalries in local government bureaucracy have also discouraged planners from claiming too wide a role in social engineering or community welfare and have forced them back to a narrowly defined technical expertise in administering state regulations and managing aspects of the land development process. Harrison (1975) studied the discussions and debates of professional planners – in RTPI meetings – in the period 1947–71, and concluded that their primary preoccupations were with technical, legal and administrative issues, and with conservation or amenity, with very little time indeed (a maximum of 5 per cent of meetings in any five-year period) devoted to social planning.

The curricula and staffing of British planning schools appears to have reflected the concerns and self-images of the profession at large. Until the 1960s there were at most five planning schools at any time, and many of the lecturers were also engaged in consultancy (either as architects or planners). They tended to see their task as the imparting of skills needed by planners, rather than the development of a critique of professional practice (Thomas 1979). From the 1960s there was an explosion of planning education; in

1964 there were eleven planning schools offering courses recognised by the RTPI, increasing to eighteen in 1970 and twenty-nine in 1975. This expansion coincided with significant changes in curricula. Based on detailed analysis of the structures of degree schemes in a number of institutions, Thomas (1979) argues that there was an increase in the proportion of time devoted to social science in the education of planners. This shift was associated with the spread of a more detached and somewhat critical stance towards practice by planning academics (see for example Simmie 1974), a development underpinned, one would surmise, by the growth of a cadre of career academics who had neither a sentimental nor material interest in portraying professional practice in a falsely rosy light (Thomas 1981). Yet this trend does not seem to have been associated with a specific concern about the role of planning in a racialised society. One planning school – at the then Polytechnic of Central London – appointed a black American anthropologist as head of department in the 1970s, and this may have played a part in that school's including welfare law, as well as planning and environmental law, in its undergraduate curriculum, and also lectures on the 'Black Liberation Front' (Thomas 1979: 61–2). However, this appears to have been the exception. Simmie's (1974) landmark text avows that its inspiration was the kind of questioning of planning taking place in Berkeley, California in the early 1970s – 'no plan would be produced without demands to know what it did for the blacks and the poor' (1974: xii) – yet when the book analyses British planning, its focus is firmly on social class and inequalities of income and wealth, not race or ethnicity (of which there appears to be no mention).

In practice, this narrowing of focus, the concern to undertake planning as a technical activity related to land use and development rather than as a process of social reform, has had socially conservative consequences. By not questioning the mores of the day, planners and the planning system tended to reinforce them. It must be acknowledged that not even all of the ostensible reformers of the early 'planning movement' were socially emancipated, especially from the gendered assumptions of their day. Meller (1990) notes Patrick Geddes's acceptance of the idea of society's being comprised of two spheres (the public and the private), with men being naturally better suited to activity in the one and women in the other. And if Geddes was never within the mainstream of the lobby for strengthening statutory town planning in Britain, Ward (1994: 31) points out that quite soon it was a socially conservative notion of home and family life (and the kinds of spaces needed for such a life) which held sway in the propaganda of the early 'town planning movement'. Lewis and Foord (1984) have illustrated this process in relation to the planning of new towns – often portrayed as examples of social reform – where the planned disposition of land uses (for example, the segregation of housing areas from employment areas) betrayed conservative assumptions about the social and economic roles of men and women and the nature of family life. Similarly, Hellmann (1977) has argued that architectural conceptions of the users of buildings have traditionally ignored the existence (and needs of) disabled people; that is, they have failed to recognise or question, the current exclusion of this group of people from vast areas of social and economic life. There is no evidence that planners did anything other than concur with architectural predilections in this respect. Similarly, the post-1947 planning system has had an effect on the welfare of black Britons even when they have had no direct dealings with it, simply because it has helped sustain constructions of rurality and English national identity which have been exclusionary of the non-white population. In addition, some key values – particularly those implicit within the bureaucratic organisation of the planning system – have been of particular significance in shaping the experiences of black people in their dealings with the planning process. Such dealings have occurred with increasing frequency from the 1970s, and a subsequent section of this chapter will focus on how the planning system has responded to this in the 1970s through to the 1990s.

Urban containment and New Towns

One of the central ideas of statutory planning from its inception, and of the 'town planning movement' more generally, has been urban containment and its corollary, the protection of rural areas from development (Hall *et al.* 1973; Ward 1994). It is clear from a range of research that, operationally, urban containment has been among the more successful (if not *the* most successful) British planning initiative at a national scale in the postwar period. There has been considerable debate about the implications of containment for land values, house prices and the welfare of different groups in the population (Simmie 1993) but for us an ideological implication of the focus on containment will be stressed, namely, its implicit support of a notion of a distinctive 'rural way of life'. Raymond Williams (1973) has explored the longevity of the myth of a rural idyll, or golden age, and its material bases in the social upheavals associated with the dynamics of capitalism. There is undoubtedly a mythic component in the concern of planners and politicians to preserve the countryside, but some aspects of this mythologising overlap with the crude reality of rural life today: the rural way of life which is being preserved is, in practice, one largely enjoyed by white people, and rural areas remain ones in which black people feel and are often made to feel uncomfortable and unwelcome.

As was noted earlier, Susan Smith (1989), among others, has shown how the residential segregation of black people in inner city areas, particularly in the postwar period, has led to an identification of the 'inner city' and 'urban policy' with the 'race issue'. Media coverage of urban unrest – such as that in the 1980s – has served to consolidate such identification (Burgess 1985; Husband 1982). By contrast, popular images of rurality take for granted that it is a place where white people live and work; and, in a powerfully exclusionary connection of ideas, rural (white) England is often promoted as being the very essence, the true territory, of Englishness, an idea popularised in the nineteenth century (Rose 1995). Thus, for example the 'Heart of England' Tourist Board – operating almost entirely in the rural areas of Warwickshire, Shropshire, Gloucestershire, Hertfordshire, Worcestershire and the Cotswolds – trades on the ambiguity between a symbolic and a geographic reading of its title. The significance of particular images is never fixed and Stephen Daniels (1993) illustrates how, over two centuries, Constable's landscape paintings have been recruited to support a variety of influential constructions of rurality and English identity, including in the interwar period a modernist interpretation. However, in the postwar period, he argues, the imagery of the landscape paintings was appropriated by those who feared the despoliation of rural England, a physical corruption, accompanied by what W.G. Hoskins termed the destruction of its meaning (Daniels 1993: 223). In 1970, Dedham Vale – the quintessential 'Constable Country' – was declared an Area of Outstanding Natural Beauty, and thereby afforded strict planning protection. The celebration of this designation by the magazine *Country Life* underlines that more than physical planning was at stake; everyone, the writer declared 'will recognise the Vale as the physical realisation of the ideal rural scene of every Englishman's dreams' (Daniels 1993: 224). Here was a powerful implicit test of ethnicity, of belonging: what landscapes did immigrants from Pakistan, the West Indies, India, Malta and elsewhere dream of? What landscapes did they feel comfortable being part of?

There is extensive anecdotal evidence of the discomfort and unease of black people who visit rural areas, of their being made to feel out of place by the perceptions of others who clearly think they *are* out of place (for example Coster 1992). Occasionally, underlying or background assumptions about who belongs are promoted to the foreground, as in two examples of local resentment when 'quintessential' English villages have become places of pilgrimage for devotees of non-Christian religions (Elveden, Suffolk, for Sikhs – see Jess and Massey (1995) – and, as was noted in Chapter 2, Bhaktivedanta Manor, Hertfordshire for Hindus – see BBC (1994)). However, we must take care not to become so excited by the idea of cultural significance of rurality for a particular conception of Englishness that we overlook its connection to the very crude racism which can infect rural areas (see for example Derounian 1993). Jay (1992) examined racism in the rural south-west of England. He found a serious problem of racism and discrimination, and suggested the following explanation:

> No doubt it derives from what an Anglican diocesan bishop in the region called the 'mind-set' of local people: some genuine ignorance, conservative resistance to the arrival of all incomers (strengthened by the recession and high unemployment), and an uncritical acceptance of

popular media stereotypes, which portray black people *per se* as a threat to British culture, jobs, housing and public order. But those are only some of the ingredients. What unquestionably exacerbates the problem by reinforcing local prejudice is the presence in the region of large numbers of white migrants from other regions who regard themselves as refugees from multiracialism. In the approving words of a county councillor and college governor:

'People have come here because they want to get away from the problems caused by the coloureds.'

The migrants themselves make no bones about it; many will openly boast. 'We've moved here to be rid of the blacks'. Their racism (which they now feel they can express much more freely than when they lived in London or the Midlands) has a chilling effect on the climate throughout the south-west; it hardens attitudes, and make changes even more difficult.

(Jay 1992: 22)

There is survey evidence which shows that recreational facilities in the countryside are less likely to be used by people from multi-racial neighbourhoods in cities than almost any other group of people. Ashcroft (1992) cites a survey by the Countryside Commission describing the sort of neighbourhood visitors to the countryside are from. Poverty, lack of private transport and sheer distance from the countryside will play an important part in keeping black people away, but seem unlikely to be the whole story given the discrepancy in his findings between 'less well-off council estates' and 'multiracial areas', with the latter less likely to provide visitors to the countryside. Malik (1992) has suggested that a complex mix of factors explains findings of a continuum of intensity of usage of countryside recreation with poor inner city Asian residents least likely to visit the countryside, their white neighbours more likely to do so, affluent Asian suburbanites visiting still more often, and white suburbanites making most use of countryside recreation. Income seems an important explanatory variable, but ethnicity also comes into play, and Malik reports that a number of respondents in interview expressed unease about 'standing out' in the countryside, though the general level of racism experienced was less than in their home town. Inevitably, racism will at times involve attempts to use the planning system to exclude black people, as in the case of the Indian applicant for planning permission documented by the Commission for Race Equality in a Yorkshire village and reported in Krishnarayan and Thomas (1993: 23) There need be no suggestion that the planning system, or planners (individually or collectively) willed a racialised countryside, but the professional and political concern for urban containment and preservation of the 'character' of rural areas which has been a strong and consistent thread through postwar planning has played an important ideological and practical role in sustaining

racial segregation, not just of residence (which has relied on other mechanisms as well) but of 'way of life' more generally.

A similar point could be made in relation to another postwar planning
initiative which, periodically, grabbed both political and planning imaginations, namely the creation of New Towns. Available evidence suggests that
New Towns tended not to provide opportunities for black and ethnic
minorities, not because of direct discrimination but rather because the
mechanisms by which residents arrived in New Towns were not ones to
which black and ethnic minorities had as much access as the population in
general. For the first two postwar decades, there was no official recognition
that Britain's changing multi-racial character might have implications for the
composition of New Towns. Aldridge's (1979: 31) judgement on the 1946
Reith Committee report is that its concern with 'social balance' had a very
specific meaning: 'The main meaning of "balance" therefore is unequivocal:
it is class balance, both in terms of income group and status'. There is no
evidence that this changed until the late 1960s, when some New Town corporations began to take active steps to disseminate information about
opportunities in New Towns to ethnic minorities (Deakin and Ungerson
1973). By then, 'race relations' was a high-profile political issue, and it had
become clear that black and ethnic minorities were under-represented in
New Towns (Deakin and Ungerson 1977: viii). A series of studies of migration
to new and expanding towns produced no evidence of direct racial discrimination, but it did seem that the channels by which new residents reached
them were more accessible to young skilled white working-class residents
than to others. These were not only formal channels, where the offer of a
New Town home tended to be linked to the movement of one's employer to
the area, but also informal channels; Thomas (1969) suggested that most
migrants to New Towns had to find jobs there outside the various schemes
promoted by development corporations. Ethnic minorities living in the inner
city tended not to be employed in the kinds of manufacturing firms relo-
cating to New Towns and were already suffering from discrimination in the
employment market, which provided no real incentive to travel to a New
Town in the hope (or expectation) of finding work. Indeed, some observers
in the 1970s speculated that ethnic minorities were reluctant to move to New
Towns, even when encouraged to do so, because of their nervousness about
race relations outside areas with which they had grown accustomed (Deakin
and Ungerson 1977). More tangible were the reasons of Asians for not
leaving inner London; Deakin and Ungerson's study of the early 1970s
pointed out that a large proportion of Asian immigrants had entered owner-
occupation of housing as the best way of improving their housing
conditions, given the difficulties they faced in being allocated public housing
(1977: 159). Their owner-occupation, however, gave them a financial stake
and financial tie which those in rented housing did not have. They reported
a marked reluctance among Asian owner-occupiers to consider moving to

new or expanded towns. In their study of Harlow New Town, Wrench *et al.* (1993: 11) claim that many of that town's residents (white and non-white) still perceive Harlow as a town built for whites, a perception to be found also in other New Towns. The reality, however, is that by the 1990s some New Towns, such as Milton Keynes and Harlow, have proportionately as many ethnic minority residents as the country as a whole; but they are 'invisible minorities', their existence and experience of racial discrimination disavowed by local government, the police and private sector employers.

Urban containment and the development of New Towns were among the more prominent of postwar British planning's national policies. For most of this period, however, they were promoted with a very limited (and some-times non existent) conception of the implications of planning initiatives for the welfare of the population at large, or specific segments of it. The general view seems to have been that planning was a 'good thing', ensuring a better quality of life and greater economic activity, but with virtually no research to make these claims more precise (or, indeed, to substantiate them). Reade's judgement in relation to the claimed beneficial effect of planning is that: 'Professional planners themselves...have produced virtually no...down-to-earth knowledge of it' (1987: 84). It is scarcely surprising, then, that planning's contribution to racial injustice has been overlooked.

Bureaucratisation

The bureaucratisation of the planning system, particularly postwar, has served to reinforce its insulation from the realities of a society where race is related to social and economic inequalities, and the political struggles arising from that. The comprehensive state-run planning system set up in Britain in 1947 has dominated the ethos of the planning profession ever since, simply because most members of the RTPI are local government employees. As a number of commentators have noted, the postwar planning system has mediated between competing interests: landowners, various fractions of capital and others (Hague 1984; Healey *et al.* 1988). In this fraught environ-ment, planners have come to recognise the utility of a number of bureaucratic values which can help them define a useful role for themselves, while being shielded from the instability – personal and professional – asso-ciated with political infighting. In particular, a reliance on *formality* is useful; in other words, a depersonalisation of interactions with others in the system, which involves *inter alia* formal recording of agreements, representa-tions and so on and a formal equality of treatment (Weber 1948). Stereotypical planners ask those with whom they deal to 'put it in writing' (so there is a formal record of the communication) and are constantly reminding local politicians that the personal circumstances of an applicant for planning permission are irrelevant in deciding it. This same ethos pervades all aspects of planning. These bureaucratic working practices help explain resistance among planners to the idea of positive action to overcome any disadvantage black people might be suffering within, and at the hands of, the planning system. The initial widespread reaction is that the scrupulous bureaucratic formality which planners have perfected over decades is a guarantee that there will be no racial discrimination exercised within the planning system. The system, being depersonalised, is 'colour blind'; and any attempt to modify that principle will threaten the integrity of the planning system itself and create practical difficulties in the working lives of planners. This line of reasoning is illustrated by a report produced jointly by the RTPI and the Commission for Racial Equality (CRE) in 1983, which lists some of the common reactions in the profession to calls for action to secure race equality within the planning system:

- we treat everybody the same, regardless of race, thus avoiding any possibility of discrimination;
- it is our policy not to discriminate on racial grounds, and therefore none of our planning measures discriminate against black people;
- although we do what we can to assist racial minorities, we must recognize that we run the risk of discrimination against white people, which is just as bad.

(RTPI/CRE 1983: 15–16)

The significance of these comments will be discussed in Chapter 4.

It appears that studies such as that of Rex and Moore, of housing in Sparkbrook, Birmingham, or the lessons of public sector housing allocation discussed earlier in the chapter, have had little impact on professional attitudes among planners. The foregoing discussion suggests that there are factors which will tend to inhibit the responsiveness of the planning system to arguments calling for positive action for securing racial equality, and will also lead it to a tendency to reflect poplar stereotypes and racial ideologies. On the other hand, within the British planning system strong political pressures at local or national level can overcome professional reservations or self-interest. The next section considers the response of the planning system to precisely such pressures, which came to the fore (in at least some localities) from the 1970s onwards; and also its response to the forceful New Right philosophy of Conservative national governments after 1979, which were deeply sceptical of race equality initiatives.

Planning and race in the 1970s

From the late 1960s and through the 1970s, the racialisation of British politics and society pressed in on planning in two ways. First, as was noted earlier, British urban policy became overtly racialised; in particular, from the late 1960s urban policy, especially the Urban Programme (UP), reflected

and consolidated the identification of the black and ethnic minority population as a problem, as constituting a set of 'special needs' which required
additional public funding. However, by the late 1970s the 'inner city' was not
simply a focus of racialised social problems, but was also a site of economic
decline and a symbol of 'yesterday's economy'. The 1977 White Paper,
'Policy for the Inner Cities', identified the inner city as the victim of
economic restructuring and promoted the idea of coordinated public sector
action (inner area 'partnerships') to create places which could be attractive
for investment once more. The core of the approach, to deploy terminology
popularised in the 1980s, was to facilitate restructuring for capital (that is,
economic restructuring on the terms of largely unfettered investment flows).
In the 1980s this approach was to be interpreted even more narrowly as a
focus on property development and spatial restructuring which would facilitate reinvestment by capital, with the benefits eventually trickling down to
the population at large (Healey *et al.* 1992; Imrie and Thomas 1993). This
was not a politically radical agenda. As a result, it is perhaps to be expected
that combating racism and racial disadvantage did not loom large in the
concerns of inner city policy.

This is not to deny that some benefits of urban policy flowed to black
and ethnic minority residents. Munt's judicious evaluation of urban policy
to the late 1980s is that:

> it would be an over simplification to suggest that black people have not
> benefited from the range of urban initiatives. However, the overwhelming
> impression, for data are limited, is that the benefits accruing to black
> communities have been incidental rather than intrinsic within urban
> policy and have been confined to individual projects.
>
> (1994: 155)

Moreover, while individual urban policy initiatives might have been related
explicitly to the needs of black and ethnic minorities, urban policy as a
whole has never acknowledged the complexity of racism and racial discrimination. Munt demonstrates how shifts in central government priorities
within the UP from largely revenue-based social projects to capital-based
economic projects in effect tended to exclude non-statutory black organisations from UP funding, a consequence which was both unremarked and
unanticipated.

For planners, then, there was little *national* pressure to ponder the significance of social disadvantage, and the profession's own ethos, as we have
seen, militated against importing issues of distributive justice and social
welfare more generally into 'technical' activities. Nevertheless, we can surmise
(in the absence of comprehensive evidence) that there were significant variations
from place to place in the way race entered discussions about planning. The

next section of the chapter illustrates this by considering the experiences of two areas.

In the late 1970s, it appears that some of the distinctive uses of, and demands made upon, the built environment by (particularly) Asian communities led to some urban local authorities devising policies to guide the consideration of planning applications for proposals such as places of worship or house extensions. A typical example of such a policy is found in a report of the Directorate of Technical Services to Kirklees Borough Council (West Yorkshire) in 1981, which discussed the question of how to resolve the continued difficulties being encountered in satisfying the need for religious establishments serving the Muslim community (Kirklees MBC 1981). In an appendix, the report identifies five other local authorities which had explicitly addressed the same issue in recent years. The concerns of the Kirklees planners seem typical of those of other authorities. In essence, they focused on how to reconcile the large demand for (often small) mosques from quite poor communities, with their professional concerns that 'nuisance' be avoided. 'Nuisance' was measured in a fashion typical of the planning system, in an entirely subjective though not necessarily arbitrary manner, which almost guaranteed an ethnocentric approach. In effect, as with the consideration of hot food takeaways (Thomas and Thomas 1990), an overwhelmingly white, middle-class profession was defining what constituted 'nuisance', seemingly oblivious to the possibility of there being systematically different perceptions among the population at large. The ideal solution advocated by Kirklees in relation to places of worship was to use only detached properties where some off-street parking could be provided, but such properties could be expensive. The report bears eloquent testimony to the clash of cultures and values, as a profession which has struggled to gain legitimacy as the arbiter of adequate environmental standards faces new demands on the built environment which involve ways of life and attitudes with which it (the profession) is largely unfamiliar. The result was an uneasy compromise: a continued preference for detached premises, but an acceptance that, in certain circumstances, conversion or changing the use of properties which are not ideally suitable may be contemplated. This would respect the importance of religious facilities to the Muslim community and recognise the fact that smaller, localised communities may experience difficulty in finding premises which are ideally suitable as places of worship. In responding to this situation, some other authorities approached (and continue to approach) the issue by seeing the use of less than ideal property as a temporary measure. Accordingly, unlimited permissions are not recommended as it is felt that council policy needs to remain flexible, and the ultimate return of premises to their original use should be encouraged.

Apart from illustrating the tensions which some authorities were evidently experiencing as they found themselves operating in a multi-cultural society, the Kirklees example is also useful in showing how race or ethnicity often entered local planning authorities' deliberations. In essence, it registered as a 'problem', actual or potential, as a phenomenon which was causing difficulties for the planning system. We can surmise that at least some planners, and local councillors, would have considered the problematic nature of planning in a racialised society to be simply one aspect of the general problem caused by the presence of numbers of black people in the country. Yet the kind of planning issue addressed in the Kirklees report is not unique. Changing social and economic conditions, for example, patterns of leisure or retailing, regularly require a reappraisal of planning policies. It is that process which the Kirklees report illustrates and which was also under way in a limited number of local authorities elsewhere at that time. What was *not* going on was a wholesale reappraisal of the appropriateness of existing planning policies *and* procedures to the realities of a multi-racial or multi-cultural society. A response such as Kirklees was a pragmatic one to a particular 'problem', not a rethinking based on an acceptance of the possibility of far-reaching racial discrimination or disadvantage.

The experience of Leicester City Council illustrates how the narrowly professional response to the needs of black and ethnic minorities could be broadened if there were sufficient political pressure to do so. In the late 1970s Leicester's planners, like those in Kirklees and elsewhere, found themselves dealing with increasing numbers of planning applications for places of worship. As Farnsworth (1989: 19) puts it, 'Leicester's 1977 policy saw each place of worship as a potential nuisance to nearby residents'. Since then, however, there has been a more considered planning response, not only in relation to places of worship but to ethnic minority needs and aspirations more generally. Notably, the ethnic origin of applicants for planning permission has been monitored throughout the 1980s (and into the 1990s) so that systematic data could be collected on whether one important 'output' or 'outcome' of the planning system was distributed disproportionately to some ethnic groups rather than others. The findings of Leicester's monitoring will be discussed in Chapter 4, but its introduction, appraisal and refinement over more than a decade (Leicester City Council 1992) is presented here as evidence of how local planning authorities can move beyond a simple conception of ethnic minorities as a set of nuisances.

It is clear from Farnsworth's (1989) review of Leicester's initiatives that, whatever the limitations of individual efforts, in the 1980s the planning department was reappraising many aspects of its operation to see whether, unwittingly, they were racially discriminatory. Going beyond this, the question was asked as to whether there was positive action the department could take to counter some of the effects of racial discrimination in society at large. In 1985, two trainee planners of Asian origin were appointed as part of a council-wide positive action initiative to increase the disproportionately small ethnic minority presence in its workforce (Nallamilli 1989).

Though those initiatives depended upon the cooperation of planning officers (especially senior officers) for their introduction, it is also clear that the City Council was corporately committed to countering racism, and that there was a political will to see action across all the authority's activities (Farnsworth 1989). Though the evidence is anecdotal, such political vision seems to be vital in shifting planners from a reactive and negative stance to a more positive approach which recognises that taking the racialisation of society (and consequent racism) seriously means reappraising every aspect of the planning authority's working practices (Ahmed and Booth 1994; Thomas and Krishnarayan 1993).

Conclusion

This chapter has surveyed the hesitant response of the British planning system to the racialisation of politics and public policy. A number of authoritative commentators on British planning in the last ninety years have noted the influence wielded over it by the planning profession (Reade 1987: 216; Healey *et al.* 1988: 225–43), the agriculture and mineral extraction industries (Healey *et al.* 1988), and well-organised pressure groups, especially those representing property interests, including better-off residents' groups in suburban and rural areas (Healey *et al.* 1988). These influences which have shaped the contours of the overall system are mediated at local level by specific local configurations of power relations (for example, Gilg and Kelly 1996). The overall result has been that the planning system's consequences have tended to be socially regressive (Blowers and Pain 1999: 290). The chapter has sketched how the interests of at least some of these groups (notably, professional planners and better off residents of rural areas) seemed to be served by planning ideologies and practices which did not question the role of planning in a racialised society. However, in the 1970s and 1980s the needs of black and ethnic minority residents forced them into greater contact with the planning system; in addition, politicians and community activists in some areas became more aware of the existence and significance of planning. In these circumstances, the planning system in certain places has responded positively. Chapter 4 will review evidence of how far this sensitivity and positive response had extended by the 1990s.

Planning in a racialised society
Britain in the 1990s

Introduction

This chapter considers the available evidence about the sensitivity of the British planning system to a particular feature of its social context, namely, its being part of a racialised society (that is, one characterised by the use of the category of race as a way of classifying, explaining and judging social behaviour and personal – and communal – worth). A major part of the chapter examines the results of surveys of the sensitivity of planning authorities to the needs and aspirations of black and ethnic minorities. While it can be argued that these surveys suffered from a conceptual confusion between race and ethnicity (Ratcliffe 1998; Thomas 1997), they still shed useful light on the operation of the planning system. The latter part of the chapter considers some of the implications of the 'modernising local government' agenda of the current government for race equality and planning.

The surveys which are discussed give an authoritative picture of planning practice from the late 1980s onwards, but before looking at them it should be noted that since 1983 there has been clear advice for all those involved in 'Planning for a Multi-Racial Britain' (RTPI/CRE: 1983). Over fifteen years after its publication, the eighty or so pages of the report of a joint RTPI/CRE working party still provide an excellent starting point for considering what the various participants in the planning system need to do to try to ensure it operates fairly in a society infected by racially based unfairness and inequality. Its thirty-six recommendations recognise that planning is a complex mix of policy processes and consequently that while action is required by professionals (and their Institute), there is also a need for complementary and supportive action by local authorities (corporately and as planning authorities), by the CRE and local race equality councils, by central government, and by political parties. However, the detailed recommendations do not obscure a central message of the report – one which in a sense, its very existence proclaims – that all those involved in planning need to take seriously the proposition that the planning process is both affected by and can itself influence the racialised society within which it operates. In an early chapter, the report notes that 'this working party has repeatedly found town planning and racial minorities engaged in a dialogue of the deaf' (RTPI/CRE 1983: 13). It lists a number of what it calls 'fallacies and misconceptions' (1983: 15) it came across in its discussions with professionals, which were used to justify a lack of engagement with discussions and debate about racial equality for a variety of reasons (1983: 15–17). A few were listed in Chapter 3, but they are worth repeating as a bloc:

'We treat everybody the same way, regardless of race, thus avoiding any possibility of discrimination.'
'It is our policy not to discriminate on racial grounds and therefore none of our planning measures discriminate against black people.'
'Race is a sensitive subject. It is better to avoid explicit policies and procedures. We are quietly getting on with it, taking as sympathetic a view as possible, without making a fuss.'
'Although we do what we can to assist racial minorities, we must recognise that we run the risk of discrimination against white people, which is just as bad.'
'There is no need to take any special steps in our area, since there are hardly any black people.'
'Black people are not the only disadvantaged group. They will benefit from special measures aimed at alleviating unemployment, social deprivation, etc. and should not be singled out over and above other disadvantaged groups.'
'In the current financial climate there are little or no resources to meet the needs of racial minorities even if we wanted to.'
'Black peoples' planning needs are no different from anyone else's.'
'Even if we recognised their special needs there is nothing that town planners can do about them, we don't have the powers.'

(RTPI/CRE 1983: 15–17).

Each of these is carefully (and rather sensitively) rebutted. The core arguments are that if some ethnic minorities have needs relevant to planning which are systematically different from those of others in the population, then to ignore them (to operate in a 'colour blind' fashion) is to engage in unfairness amounting to discrimination. Moreover, when racial discrimination – direct and indirect – has been shown to exist in services such as housing, then planners need to be sensitive to its possibility in their services. Finally, planning is subject to the Race Relations Act, and planners have a professional duty to be aware of its implications for their work. These points are as valid now as they were then. They make, it should be noted, a rather conservative case for equality of opportunity (see Chapter 1): a call for a fair playing field, no positive discrimination, no redress of the accumulated disadvantage of previous oppression; and this is a case which should be acceptable by Conservative or New Labour governments (and die-hard professionals) concerned about providing a good service to *all* clients and citizens (see Thomas and Krishnarayan 1993).

This point is driven home in an equally careful discussion which follows of what is meant by 'positive action', and why it can be both fair and consistent with well-established principles of good planning practice. It bears quotation at length:

> Positive action involves special treatment for those in a disadvantaged position (with regard to access to facilities or services) so that they obtain *equal* opportunities. It does not involve giving additional help so that the disadvantaged move to an especially favoured position.
>
> Positive action is widespread in town planning, although traditionally it occurred in relation to land areas rather than particular social groups. Thus people living in National Parks, Areas of Outstanding Natural Beauty and Conservation Areas benefit from especially rigorous control over development, design and environmental standards. Those in General Improvement Areas (GIAs) qualify for extra housing improvement subsidies and various environmental benefits; and commercial developers in enterprise zones are less subject to planning controls than is normally the case. There may well be scope for this type of area action to benefit black people, especially if a special element is built in to ensure equality of opportunity.
>
> Legitimate positive action is possible to meet the special needs of black people, through a combination of special measures justified on non-racial grounds and others designed to ensure access to services on the basis of equal opportunity.
>
> (RTPI/CRE 1983: 17–18)

The report is sensitive to the lessons to be learnt from housing policy and other areas of public policy, but is careful to relate them to the concerns of planners and planning. If it has a weakness, it is that it provides no intermediate step between elaborating its central theme and listing its detailed recommendations; there is no clear identification of priorities or a step-by-step action plan for those wishing to secure change. As they stand, the recommendations can appear extraordinarily daunting; moreover, particularly important suggestions are not highlighted. For example, the report recommends that:

> Local planning authorities should monitor the impact of their policies on racial minorities.
>
> (RTPI/CRE 1983: 82)

To implement section 71 of the Race Relations Act 1976 each local authority should ensure that one of its committees has overall responsibilities for race relations: that there be a chief officer designated for the authority as a whole and a senior officer within each department with officer responsibilities for race relations matters.

(RTPI/CRE 1983: 82)

The Secretary of State for the Environment should require new town and urban development corporations to make regular public reports on the steps they have taken to promote equality of opportunity for racial minorities in terms of population and employment structure in their areas.

The Secretary of State for the Environment after appropriate consultation should encourage good planning practice by issuing a Development Control Policy Note on development relating to the special needs of racial minorities in general, and places of worship and cultural assembly in particular. He should also review the training and advice given on race relations to the Department's Planning Inspectorate.

(RTPI/CRE 1983: 84)

However, these far-reaching recommendations were mixed with rather well-meaning but somewhat anodyne ones enjoining 'Town Planners [to] continually reassess their attitudes, professional advice and practice to see if racial discrimination is occurring as a result of these' (RTPI/CRE 1983: 81) or 'The Institute's Council [to] be encouraged to increase contact between planning aid workers and racial minorities' (RTPI/CRE 1983: 81). Later in this chapter a graduated approach to promoting race equality is set out, which contrasts with this apparent 'all or nothing' stance.

Yet these limitations do not detract from the landmark status of the report. Some four years in preparation, it contained more than enough guidance for anyone involved in the planning system who wanted to take race equality seriously.

Yet perhaps the most significant conclusions of surveys of local planning authorities conducted in the 1990s is, first, their unwillingness to take seriously the possibility that their operations might be unfair to black and ethnic (that is, typically racialised) minorities, whether this amounts to illegal discrimination or not; and, second, the persistence of this apparent complacency. In terms of Rees's (1998) three-part model of promoting equal opportunities (of which more later), planning authorities seem to be stuck at the stage of simply insisting that they are treating everyone equally, though too often with too little hard evidence, even of that.

Why there has been negligible change over fifteen years or more is a question addressed later in this chapter. The discussion identifies the kinds of factors which constrain organisational change in local government, and also sets the activities of planning authorities in a wider context: bureaucratic and technical policy processes are important, but are only some of the strands which constitute the planning system. The chapter ends by looking at the prospects for change opened up by the 'modernising planning' agenda of the 1997 Labour government. In particular, it analyses the scope for exploiting Best Value as a way of 'mainstreaming' race equality within the planning system.

Planning surveyed

Surveys of planning authorities were conducted in 1988, 1992, 1993 and 1997/8 with a view to establishing their sensitivity to operating in a multi-ethnic and racialised society. The results have been reported fully and remain accessible (Davies n.d.; Krishnarayan and Thomas 1993; Loftman and Beazley 1998a, 1998b; Owen 1989), so only a selective review is presented in this chapter. A key issue is that identified by the 1983 RTPI/CRE report: to what extent are planning authorities aware of the possibility of racial discrimination infecting the planning system? To what extent do they think through the implications of operating a planning system in a society beset by racial inequality, or do they simply view planning as somehow insulated from what goes on in the wider society?

On the basis of analyses such as those of Krishnarayan and Thomas (1993), it is plausible to suggest that certain institutional responses (procedures) are good indicators of the degree of organisational sensitivity to the possibility of racial discrimination in planning. They single out the following:

*   ethnic monitoring, particularly of the outputs of the planning process. Monitoring provides systematically collected data about the distribution of the outcomes of planning (costs *and* benefits). A distribution steered towards particular groups is not *conclusive* evidence of discrimination, but is an indication that there may be some systematic bias, and that further, more sophisticated investigation is required. Monitoring outcomes by ethnicity is a simple acknowledgement of the possibility of racially based unfairness. Of course, monitoring alone prevents nothing; its results must feed into the management of planning.
*   the flagging up, in reports to planning committees of the implications of their content and recommendations for various racialised or other groups. This device acknowledges that planning decisions may well have a differential impact on different groups, and that in a society characterised by social inequality it is possible to perpetuate it by simply overlooking certain racialised groups.

- the existence of formal guidance for planning officers as to how to deal with racist representations (on planning applications or as part of other consultation procedures). Such guidelines acknowledge the reality of day to day racism and how it can impact on planning and, by their very existence, make it clear that racism is unacceptable and cannot simply by ignored (a tendency among some planning authorities, according to the 1983 RTPI/CRE report).
- the existence of a departmental action plan to promote race equality. If racism and racial discrimination is a real possibility in the planning system, then an action plan must surely be needed to identify more accurately the likelihood and/or existence of it and take appropriate action.

How do planning authorities measure up in relation to these indicators? Table 4.1 provides a bare summary of the findings of four surveys of local planning authorities conducted in the decade from 1987:

- a survey of all shire and metropolitan districts, conducted in 1987 (Owen 1989);
- a study commissioned by the RTPI in 1992, which focused on areas with above average proportion of ethnic minorities (but included counties where at least one district satisfied the criterion) (Krishnarayan and Thomas 1993);
- a study of all local planning authorities in the South-West of England conducted by the RTPI's branch ethnic minority liaison officer (Davies n.d.);
- a study of all local planning authorities in England, Scotland and Wales commissioned by the Local Government Association (LGA) in 1997 (Loftman and Beazley 1998a).

Given the different kinds of samples and the differences in the precise wordings of questionnaires, nothing should be read into variations of a few percentage points here and there. Indeed, there is no real temptation to discuss subtle variations, for they are submerged under an overwhelming impression of persistent general indifference or insensitivity to race equality. In their 1997 survey, Loftman and Beazley asked local planning authorities to rate the importance they attached to 'addressing race/ethnic minority issues', on a scale of 1–7, where 1 was 'not at all important' and 7 was 'very important'. Forty-five per cent of responding authorities gave a rating of 1 or 2; 13 per cent gave 6 or 7 and a further 11 per cent gave a 5 (Loftman and Beazley 1998a: 27).

Such a finding is difficult to interpret in isolation, as the response will depend upon who answered the postal questionnaire and their interpretation of what a 'race/ethnic minority issue' might be. But taken with the results

Table 4.1 Key findings of surveys of local planning authorities

Activity	Nos and % of LPAs undertaking these activities			
	1987	1992*	1993**	1997***
Ethnic monitoring of planning applicants	I	13 (14%)	(0%)	18 (7%)
Race equality implications flagged up in reports.	N/A	12 (14%)	3 (7%)	N/A
Formal guidance on racist representation†	N/A	2††	N/A	(20%)
Departmental race equality action plans	N/A	18 (20%)	N/A	(9%)

Notes:
* 135 LPAs in sample; response rate 69% (90 usable responses)
** 55 LPAs in sample; response rate 76% (45 usable responses)
*** 436 LPAs in sample; response rate 64% (277 usable responses)
† authorities responsible for d.c. only
†† from a small sub-sample
N/A question not asked

reported in Table 4.1, it seems reasonable to conclude that with a few notable exceptions British planning authorities have continually failed to perceive the relevance of concerns about racial discrimination or racial inequality for their work, despite a pioneering report in 1983 and considerable subsequent activity by the RTPI.

It is important to distinguish the suggestion that local planning authorities are insensitive to the implications for planning of operating in a racialised, and racially unjust, society from the proposition that local planning authorities are insensitive to the needs of ethnic minorities. One of the problems with the Loftman and Beazley survey question discussed above is that it obscures this distinction. Local planning authorities can be rather good at responding to the land use implications of social and economic change, if these present themselves in certain ways. So, for example, in Chapter 3 we have noted how in the 1970s a number of local planning authorities found themselves dealing with a spate of planning applications for, or complaints about, places of worship for minority ethnic groups. Their typical response was to draw up guidelines or policies setting down criteria by which to decide such applications consistently (and, it was hoped, manifestly fairly) (Thomas and Krishnarayan 1994). Such authorities were certainly responding to ethnic minorities needs. Yet they rarely went further than a single issue response. For example, they did not try to understand more fully the lives of these minorities in order to better appreciate the significance of cross-cutting distinctions such as gender and class within them, or their often distinctive use of the built and natural environment, their aspirations, their perceptions of organisations such as planning author- ities and their experiences (collectively and individually) of racial discrimination and racism. These kinds of studies, if they had been under- taken, would surely lead to a thoroughgoing reappraisal of how planning authorities related to the population of their areas, a reappraisal which would have to take into account the reality of racial discrimination within bureaucracies of all kinds.

Nevertheless, individual policy responses are not unimportant. Certainly a lack of even *ad hoc* planning responses to the needs of ethnic minorities would, in a racialised society, be *prima facie* evidence of racial injustice within the planning system. Evidence from the surveys mentioned earlier in this chapter suggests that planning authorities have tended to be more ready to make *ad hoc* responses to something they could define as a planning problem, rather than consider how planning processes might reinforce (or challenge) processes of racial discrimination and racial disadvantage. Krishnarayan and Thomas (1993: 50) recorded one-third of their respondents (thirty authorities) claiming to have planning policies reflecting the particular needs of black and ethnic minorities. Over two-thirds of these authorities had policies relating to places of worship or community facilities; the next most popular topic for policies was housing (with seven local authorities having policies which referred to two specific housing needs of black and ethnic minority people). Other topics which feature in such policies were employment (four authorities), safety and security in design (three), increased participation in leisure (one) and the reten- tion of specialised shops (one).

Five years later, Loftman and Beazley (1998a: 26) found thirty-seven local planning authorities claiming to have planning policies which specifically related to the needs of black and ethnic minority communities. As a propor- tion of their responses, this thirty-seven amounted to only 13 per cent, but the proportions are not significant here. The 1992 survey was of areas with relatively large black and ethnic minority populations while the 1997 survey included all local planning authorities; but policy responses have a strong correlation with the size of the black and ethnic minority population (Loftman and Beazley 1998a: 26). This is because local planning authorities view the lives of black and ethnic minorities, if they consider them at all, as potential influences on patterns of land use; their perspective is embedded in the planning process, and they look out from there. They do not, in general, analyse the society of which planning is a part and then consider what effects this context may have on planning (for example, can racism and racial discrimination seep into planning processes?) and what influence may planning have on its social context (does planning play its part in racial formation, and can planning play a part in challenging racialisation?). One of the great hopes which some have for the innovation in local government known as Best Value is that it will provide an impetus for dislodging this view 'from the inside looking out' (Thomas and Lo Piccolo 1999).

Beginning to appreciate how the planning system is viewed by its users, however they are defined, depends upon establishing a dialogue with them. The RTPI/CRE report (1983) was scathing about the absence of constructive communication between planning authorities and ethnic minority groups. Ten years later, Krishnarayan and Thomas (1993: 68) concluded that 'for most planning authorities, contact with black and ethnic minority organisations is episodic and fragmentary'. They came across innovative procedures, such as regular 'community forums' where black and ethnic minority residents could bring their grievances or comments (defined in their own terms) and discuss them with a range of local authority officers and members (so there was no need for the residents to try to work out if their problems were, in bureaucratic terms, planning problems, housing problems or whatever). But there seemed to be more examples, even among those authorities who tried to set up dialogues, of a reluctance to view their innovations as more than a way of assisting planners to get the job done. Thus du Boulay (1989) reported on attempts by planners in Coventry to set up a consultation forum, but also to control its agenda and constitution. Understandably, this met resistance from community groups concerned about being manipulated.

This attempt to simultaneously open up aspects of the planning process to public comment, or even purported public influence, while trying to retain control for either planning professionals or the planning authority has bedevilled the history of public participation in British planning (Damer and Hague 1971; Thomas 1996). It has manifested itself graphically in the day to day experiences of specialist officers appointed in planning departments to liaise with ethnic minority communities and/or advise on planning issues as they affect ethnic minorities.[1] As such posts remain an important if relatively unusual feature of planning departments (Loftman and Beazley 1998a), the way they were used in the early 1990s still sheds useful light on the institutional context within which race equality has been pursued in British planning. Krishnarayan and Thomas (1993: 71) interviewed seven of the eight people they had come across in such posts, and examined relevant departmental documentation.

Some posts were created as responses to 'difficulties' which the local authority felt it was experiencing with local ethnic minority communities; for example, a series of awkward planning applications in which there was evident dissatisfaction among community leaders, or, more pointedly, among councillors. In that respect, the posts were an *ad hoc* response to a perceived problem, in much the same way as isolated policies on hot food takeaways or places of worship can be. Given their origin, it is perhaps not surprising that the precise role of many of the post holders was in practice uncertain and, in effect, was negotiated as they went along.

In interview, most advisers expressed the feeling that their colleagues had an ambivalent view of them. On the one hand, they wanted them to dispense instant wisdom and advice on 'ethnic dimensions' of the local authority's planning role (including at times speaking on behalf of the black and ethnic minority communities). A sentence from one authority's note on the role of such a liaison officer captured a flavour of this: 'the main duties of the post include liaison with the ethnic minorities at public participation and plan preparation stages in connection with the preparation or review of Local Plans'. The division of labour envisaged within that planning depart-ment is pretty explicit, with the liaison officer 'dealing with' ethnic minorities; to be 'normally ignored', as one jaundiced officer is reported as having said.

But on the other hand, advisers/liaison officers felt that colleagues some-times suspected them of 'taking the side of' black and ethnic minority people (for example, if they persistently drew attention to the way an ethnic minority planning applicant viewed the merits or drawbacks of his/her application). Officers without formal planning qualifications felt that this deficiency might incline planning colleagues to feel that they were being less than objective in promoting the cases from black and ethnic minority communities. However, liaison officers with professional qualifications, and indeed professionally qualified agents, also experienced these reactions from other planners, though one or two did say that being professionally qualified had helped them communicate with fellow officers and helped them to put their arguments in particular ways. In all these cases, there are assumptions of 'us' and 'them', of black and ethnic minorities as 'Other', as outside the mainstream, and of their 'sticking together' as a result. These ideas and feel-ings are endemic in British society and are measures of its racialisation, but in 1993 were not interpreted as such. (at least by most planning officers).[2]

The generally vague brief for liaison officers/race advisers often left them with scope to argue for or even pioneer new initiatives. However, as they were in general of middle rank or below within their departments (and also felt 'out of the mainstream' of the department's work), their rate of success was not always high, and there was a general disillusionment when they came to assess their impact within their department. A number referred to a lack of genuine commitment at senior levels to working through the implica-tions of equal opportunities for planning. A liaison officer who was on the departmental management team, and had the support of senior colleagues was noticeably less jaundiced in her description of her work than were some of those we interviewed.

It is tempting to consider these accounts as evidence of a special failure of the planning system. Of course, they do represent weakness of planning, and planning has its own particular and peculiar responses to operating in racialised Britain. But the argument of Chapter 3 is that its social and polit-ical context has a significant influence on the way planning operates. The characterisation of racialised minorities as problematic may owe something to the desire of professionals for a relatively quiet life, but I would argue, draws much more on the kinds of racial stereotypes noted by Solomos (1993), Smith (1985) and Burgess (1985), and discussed in Chapter 3. And it was also noted in that chapter that attempts to use liaison officers as pacifiers or defusers of troublesome residents was something found outside mainstream planning, and was most recently documented in the case of urban development corporations (Brownill *et al.* 1997)

Five years after the RTPI's commissioned study, the Local Government Association (LGA) commissioned a similar survey. The intervening years had seen increasing pressure on local authorities to view the users of their service as customers to whose requirements and experiences they had to be sensitive. While those services subject to compulsory competitive tendering (CCT) have perhaps been at the sharp end of this pressure, planning authorities have not avoided it (see for example Tewdwr-Jones and Harris 1998).

Yet Loftman and Beazley (1998a: 31) concluded that 'few LPAs have in place specific consultation and/or communication mechanisms targeted at local black and ethnic minority communities'. Fourteen per cent of responding authorities said they had such mechanisms. The kinds of mechanisms (and, indeed, the number of authorities using them) displays an extraordinary similarity to Krishnarayan and Thomas's findings of five years earlier (see Table 4.2).

In 1992, and again in 1997, it was possible to point to exemplary practice. For example, while local planning authorities in general seemed unable to grasp the necessity of ethnic monitoring, Leicester City Council has a track record of not only monitoring the ethnic background of planning applicants since the 1980s, but of taking extraordinary care over analysing the results and trying to use them to improve departmental procedures (Leicester City Council

Table 4.2 Formal consultative/communication mechanisms used by local planning authorities, 1992 and 1997, by numbers of local planning authorities

	1992	1997
Ethnic minority community forums	10	13
Ethnic minority liaison officers/race advisers	8	13
Race equality councils	8	9
Ethnic minority focus groups	0	7
Joint liaison committee of council	7	0

Source: 1992 data: Krishnarayan and Thomas (1993: 67); 1997 data: Loftman and Beazley (1998a: 31).

1992). In relation to consultation and participation, Sheffield City Council based its practices, in the 1980s and early 1990s, on an acute (and explicit) analysis of which voices were normally heard in the planning system. It then devoted resources to assisting normally excluded groups (including Asian women, for example) to formulate responses to the council's development plan proposals (Alty and Darke 1987; Krishnarayan and Thomas 1993: 121–5). A number of other authorities have also tried to ensure that in some of their practices they promote race equality (Thomas and Krishnarayan 1994; Loftman and Beazley 1998a). Yet in a sense, the existence of these examples only raises in a more insistent fashion the question of why there has been a general indifference to race equality among planning authorities. The Royal Town Planning Institute published comprehensive guidance on good practice in 1983 and 1993, and more specialised, narrowly focused advice thereafter (RTPI 1996), and this has been complemented by a number of publications aimed at planning professionals (for example Davies n.d.; Gilroy 1993; Thomas and Krishnarayan 1993, 1994). Why have they had such little apparent influence on the practices of local planning authorities?

It may be argued at this point that too dispiriting a picture is being painted; that planning is no worse than comparable governmental functions and that, in any event, little needs to be done to improve matters. It is probably unhelpful to compare planning with other areas of public policy, though the comments of Robert Moore, a doyen of social policy research and practice, in a justifiably critical (if rather snooty) review of Thomas and Krishnarayan (1994) should give some pause for thought:

> Seasoned students of 'race' relations and equal opportunities policies will find the style of discussion transports them back to an earlier history in other fields. Perhaps the collection fairly represents the current state of planning practice in the UK, in which case, so much the worse for planners.
>
> (Moore 1995: 465)

Yet trying to devise league tables of policy fields is not an especially constructive activity; it might be more helpful to try to assess how far, and in what direction, most local planning authority practice needs to travel if it is to meet the kinds of standards being advocated by those with experience of promoting equal opportunities.

Rees's (1999; ch. 6) three-stage model provides a useful framework for evaluating the progress which planning departments have made in taking race equality seriously. Reviewing twenty-five years of working towards gender equality in Wales, particularly within the labour market, Rees argues that three stages are discernible:

(1) Treating people equally. At this stage, the main concern was treating men and women equally, as required by statute. This approach tackled the most gross forms of discrimination, but was reactive; it took no account, for example, of the circumstances which might influence the way men and women (in Rees's case) presented themselves in the labour market or, by extension, within bureaucratic processes.

(2) Positive action. At this stage there was recognition that there were systematic differences between people (in Rees's examples, between men and women, in relation to training, career trajectories and so on). Some of these differences needed to be addressed if a level playing field was to be created, and so promoting equal opportunities had to involve positive action to eradicate disadvantages suffered by women (and, by extension, other groups) which could not be overcome simply by treating people equally within a given process. However, this approach took the world as it was largely as given, and tried to equip women to compete better with it. Rees's final stage involves considering the nature of organisations across the board, and tackling 'essential issues of organisational culture and practice' (Rees 1999: 91).

(3) Mainstreaming equality: this builds on an appropriate legal framework, and on positive action, but attempts to integrate promoting equality into all policies, programmes and actions of public and private services and companies. Putting matters crudely, it does not take the world as given and equip racialised ethnic minorities to 'fit in'; rather, it tries to shape a world which fits a society of diversity. So working practices and procedures are not to be devised in isolation from the needs of, say, women and/or some ethnic minority groups, or disabled people, who are then 'assisted' to cope with unfriendly practices. Rather, the impact and value of practices and procedures are considered in relation to the whole population *from the outset*; that is, at the design stage. 'Mainstreaming is the integration of equal opportunities into all policy development, implementation, evaluation and review processes' (WLGA 1999: 2). Mainstreaming, like for the radical view of promoting equal opportunities, involves questioning racialised identities and the power relations embedded in them.

This is a useful model for our purposes, not least because it can operate with a 'thin' conception of equal opportunities (see Chapter 1), the conception enjoying the broader support in Britain, including – one supposes – within the planning profession (see for example Thomas and Krishnarayan 1993). In using it we must beware, of course, of suggesting any inevitable progression from one stage to another; equal opportunities are struggled for, and reverses are as possible as advances.

Rees's idea of a potential progression finds expression in the detailed recommendations of the Commission for Racial Equality in its 'Racial

Equality means Quality', published in both London and Edinburgh (1995). The CRE identifies five levels of activity in promoting race equality as applied to various aspects of local government activity and it is evident that the progression from level 1 to level 5 is broadly from 'treating people equally' to 'mainstreaming'. The illustrations in the report are meant to apply to corporate management of services, and consequently not all the recommendations apply to specific services, such as planning. Nevertheless, enough apply to provide a measure of how the planning services of local government measure in relation to recommended best practice.

The surveys of local authorities conducted in 1992 and 1997 were not designed to establish at what level local planning authorities were to be found. Moreover, performance in any local planning authority can be patchy: there can be a mix of levels, so to speak. For this reason, the CRE recommendations are being used solely as a rough guide to how much may need to be done. As such, they provide a sobering assessment of the performance and commitment of planning authorities; the brief review of some key findings presented earlier suggests that few are even at level 2, in a hierarchy of five. This is dispiriting; but the CRE recommendations can also be read as a general prescription for a graduated approach to promoting race equality. Unlike the 'all or nothing' stance which seemed to be implicit in the 1983 CRE/RTPI report, here is encouragement to work towards a coherent set of policies and procedures at whatever level is politically acceptable or realistic at a given time. The message is that whatever circumstances an organisation finds itself in, a coherent package for promoting race equality remains feasible; moreover, whatever package of policies and procedures is currently being followed, a further progressive step can, realistically, be contemplated.

It should also be borne in mind that discussion about mainstreaming race equality *has* occurred in one or two local planning authorities. In Sheffield, for example, one of the rationales for doing away with the post of an ethnic minority liaison officer was that this would encourage the consideration of race equality as a mainstream rather than marginal issue (Krishnarayan and Thomas 1993: 72; Ahmed and Booth 1994). This should give a little encouragement to those working for change; the next section considers how such change might be promoted.

Working for change in planning

In a number of ways, planning has changed enormously in the last twenty to thirty years, (Cullingworth 1999; Ward 1994), so why has there been so little change in the importance attached to promoting race equality in most planning authorities? In this section, no more than an outline of an answer can be given, but it will be an answer which tries to be sensitive to the complexity of the forces which shape planning practice. Drawing upon a number of analyses of organisational and cultural change in local government in general, as well as planning in particular, it is possible to construct a simple model of the factors which influence the pace of change in planning authorities (see for example Hartley *et al.* 1995; Healey and Underwood 1978; Thomas 1999a). The following seem to be crucial:

External context (external to the local authority as a whole)

- economic context
- legal–political context:
  - national
  - local
- social context

Internal context

- the history of the local authority, and relations between services
- availability of resources to support particular changes
- leadership:
  - political
  - professional/managerial

These will now be discussed briefly.

In terms of the *external context* (construed, here, as the context external to the local authority as a whole), four factors are especially important. The *national politico-legal* context is important in influencing at least some aspects of planning.

Government policy is a material consideration in development control and the law (including case law) guides and constrains what planning authorities can do in relation to controlling development and development planning in particular. Successive reports have suggested that planners are anxious about the legality and/or acceptability in policy terms of including considerations relating to race equality in development control (Krishnarayan and Thomas 1993; Loftman and Beazley 1998a). Certainly, central government's well known hostility, in the 1980s, to equal opportunities as an aspect of 'loony leftism' was not an encouragement to planning authorities to innovate in this area, and it has been argued that even where, uniquely, government policy supported positive action to support a cultural community (namely Welsh speakers), local planning authorities were reluctant to place much weight on it as it was so at odds with the general drift of Conservative thinking (Thomas 1993; Lo Piccolo and Thomas n.d.). Yet this factor, while important, should not be overemphasised. For example, government policy is crucial if refusal of planning permission is contemplated and an appeal is likely; but this still allows a planning authority some leeway in being positive in relation to applications it wishes to grant. Moreover, considerable numbers of planners work outside the so-called core functions of development control and development planning (46 per cent of planners' time was taken up by such tasks in 1991; LGMB/RTPI 1992: 32). Planning authorities are engaged in work in urban regeneration, the environment, tourism and economic development, for example. It is true that in all these areas, national government policy is influential in setting frameworks (for example, in writing the guidelines for bidding for urban regeneration money), and there is little doubt that for twenty years this framework has not been supportive of the promotion of race equality (see for example Brownill and Darke 1998; Munt 1994); but neither has it forbidden planning authorities from innovating, especially if doing so in small schemes.

The spur to creative activity in defiance of an unhelpful framework is often local political pressure, which for our purposes will be distinguished from local political leadership (for which see later). The success of some civic societies and residents groups shows what can be achieved within the planning system by sustained, informed pressure, supported of course by resources (Lowe and Goyder 1983; Abram et al. 1996). It is clear that race equality (and, indeed, equal opportunities more generally) can be pushed on to local political agendas and influence local authority policy in certain circumstances (see for example Stoker and Brindley 1985; Leach 1989). However, anecdotal evidence suggests that planning appears not to have been given a great deal of attention by community activists promoting race equality. Employment, health and community safety seem to be priorities, and in this they might well be responding to the priorities of those they seek to work for. A poll of Asian and Afro-Caribbean voters conducted at the time of the 1987 election found that their four key concerns were unemployment, health and defence (shared by both groups), housing (for Afro-Caribbeans), and education (for Asians). A 1991 poll listed the five most significant issues among Asian voters as education, racial attacks, the health service, housing and immigration (Saggar 1998: 16–18). Yet, such national polls have to be treated with some caution: there is evidence that racialised minorities have concerns about their local areas which planning could help address. Thus in Bolton, a survey of Asians produced a league table of 'local issues' based on the percentage of respondents identifying them as important: crime (57 per cent); unemployment (39 per cent); facilities for children (29 per cent); housing development (23 per cent); education (23 per cent); traffic (21 per cent); racism (20 per cent); and green issues (3 per cent) (Leese and Wareing 1996). Planning could help with, at least, traffic, housing and facilities for children. Nevertheless, those wishing to agitate for policies important to racialised minorities have the difficult task of influencing national and local agendas on a range of topics; in this process, a genuine interest in matters covered by the planning system can be pushed to one side. It is also important to acknowledge that, especially in the last decade or so, central government has tried by various means to increase the influence of business over local government, especially in urban areas. This has not helped the promotion of equal opportunities.

Another important factor is the *social context* for the authority's operations. At its crudest, this may simply mean the number of black and ethnic minorities people in an area, though it extends far beyond this: for example, the local specificities of the racialisation of social relations will be important (see Chapter 2). Loftman and Beazley (1998a) argue that there is a direct relationship between what planning authorities can point to as actions targeted at, or sensitive to, black and ethnic minorities and the proportion of the population which is from black and ethnic minorities. While this may reflect an ability to translate numbers into political pressure, it may also signify the increasing difficulty of not explicitly recognising a section of the population once it passes a certain threshold. (Demography is not decisive, however; Sheffield City Council's positive policies were born of political belief, and the city's ethnic minority population is comparatively small.)

Finally, the authority's *economic context* is a crucial factor in shaping its activities as a planning authority, especially if resources for purely public sector projects is limited (as has been the case for over twenty years). Brindley *et al.* (1996) illustrates how the economic context can in general constrain the policies of planning authorities, and this is also true of policies and practices related to race equality. If private investment is deemed to be needed to implement change, then conditions must be created which will attract it; a concern for race equality (other than in the context of staving off disorders) is not an important element in creating such conditions.

Turning to the *internal context*, again, four factors appear to be important. The first two relate to the relationship between the planning department and the rest of the local authority. Is there a tradition of *strong departmentalism* in the authority (typically, associated with fiercely guarded professional boundaries)? If so, then changing the practices and ethos of a planning department will require impetus from within, which is perhaps where the professional institute's guidance can be useful. Looking at the position more positively, it means that a planning department may be in a position to innovate, even in a local authority not especially predisposed to make race equality an important issue. There were one or two examples of this reported by Krishnarayan and Thomas (1993). More usual, however, is a need for *corporate support* for innovation in service departments such as planning. Thomas and Krishnarayan argue that the corporate context is vital and that 'when an appropriate framework is in place, some significant changes can occur' (1994a: 48). This depends, however, on 'corporate centres' recognising planning as an important area for promoting race equality, and having the resources (personnel and financial) to help.

The two final internal factors relate to *leadership*, both political and professional–managerial. These factors, taken with the national political–legal context, are, perhaps, the three most important influences on change in planning.

The sensitivity of planning officers to the priorities of councillors, espe- cially senior ones, has been remarked upon in a number of studies over many years (for example Healey and Underwood 1978; Kitchen 1997). For example, it has been argued that the nervousness, not to say prejudices of local planning authorities in relation to planning applications for hot food takeaways, where many are refused, bear particularly heavily on ethnic minorities (Thomas 1994b). The commitment of senior politicians and senior officers is especially important in promoting organisational and cultural change (for example, in the decentralisation of service delivery, or the introduction of Best Value; see Hartley *et al.* (1995); Gaster (1993); Burns *et al.* (1994)). Both Krishnarayan and Thomas (1993) and Loftman and Beazley (1998a) reported that middle-ranking officers committed to sensitising planning to race equality often felt that there was no commitment at senior officer level. Doubtless, some of the senior officers would claim in turn that there was no real political will to support change. Studies of organ- isational change in local government suggest that it is most effectively managed when there is a degree of clarity on the part of both senior officers and members of what is being striven for, and of their respective roles in the process. Others take their cue from this (Hartley *et al.* 1995; Gaster 1993).

Using this model, it is possible to suggest why it is that race equality has made such little headway within local planning authorities, and also identify what needs to change if matters are to be improved. Of the factors discussed, it has been suggested that three are especially important in encouraging and shaping change, and in each case the evidence is that over the last twenty years these have developed in ways which do not encourage local planning authorities to take race equality seriously: the national polit- ical and legal context has been unsupportive, while at local level political and professional leadership has focused increasingly on performing well in nationally defined league tables, with an occasional foray into civic boost- erism (Cochrane 1993). The continuing low representation of black and ethnic minorities among councillors has not helped establish an alternative agenda for local government (see Table 4.3). In these inauspicious circum- stances, other factors could operate only sporadically and with difficulty.

This is a bleak analysis; but then the 1980s and 1990s have been bleak times for racial equality (Ball and Solomos 1990; Solomos 1993). The elec- tion of a New Labour government in 1997 provided some cause for optimism. While its broad approach to economic governance is neo-liberal, it has a professed concern about social justice, albeit one couched increas- ingly in terms of social cohesion (CSJ 1994; Levitas 1998). Its interpretation of social inclusion may amount to little more than entry into the labour

Table 4.3 Asian and Afro-Caribbean local authority councillors by party in
England, 1992

	Total	Labour	Conservative	Liberal Democrats	Independent
Afro-Caribbean men	53	48	1	3	1
Afro-Caribbean women	32	28	2	0	2
Asian men	185	160	10	7	7
Asian women	17	12	2	2	0
	287	248	15	12	10

Source: Tables 3–6 of Geddes (1993).

market (Levitas 1998; Lister 1998), but even this is a step above the dismissive (and racially tinged) discourse of the underclass (Morris 1994; Oppenheim and Harker 1996). Moreover, it has sketched a future for local government which provides a central (and powerful) role for local authorities as leaders of their communities. They will continue to work with 'social partners', notably business, but also with the voluntary sector (Blair 1998). Significantly, the impression is given in a series of Green (consultation) and White (policy) papers that local governance is about more than simply creating conditions for profitable private investment (though it *is* about that too; see for example DETR 1998a). The New Labour slogan is that local government needs to be modernised; and planning, as a major local government responsibility, has its own agenda for modernisation. This was initially set out in a ministerial statement in January 1998, which identified five major challenges:

- the European context for planning in this country;
- clearer statements of national policy for the small number of projects where decentralisation of decision making is not possible;
- effective arrangements for regional planning so that more issues can be resolved at this level;
- a continuous search for improvements in local efficiency; and
- a willingness to consider economic instruments and other modern policy tools to help meet the objectives of positive planning.

(Minister for the Regions, Regeneration and Planning 1998: 5)

Important as these issues are, it is noticeable that they do not include a concern for using the planning system to promote social justice, nor a concern about increasing public accountability through increasing public participation

(Tewdwr-Jones 1998). These may be touched on by the government's Urban Task Force (1999a, 1999b), but if so, they will be seen as means to an end: namely, stopping the drift of population from city centres to suburbs, and then to rural towns and villages. Though it contains pious statements of concern about racism, nothing in the 300-page report of the Task Force betrays a grasp of the implications of racialised social relations for creating more just (and civilised) cities (Thomas 1999b). Indeed, nothing in the modernising planning agenda as put into practice suggests that social justice or equal opportunities register at all on it (see for example DETR 1998b, 1999). An apparent commitment at a Local Government Association conference in May 1998 by Richard Caborn, then the minister responsible for planning in England, that advice would be produced to promote race equality in planning has led to no initiative. Yet, disappointing as the modernising planning agenda may be, it does overlap with the broader agenda of modernising local government. One of the innovations proposed as part of this agenda is to 'modernise' local government through 'Best Value' (indeed, the 1998 ministerial statement on modernising planning refers to Best Value). The question of whether *it* may provide a vehicle for promoting race equality within and through the work of local planning authorities will be examined as an important innovation in its own right, as well as a guide to the seriousness with which planning authorities may consider race equality issues under New Labour.

A Parliamentary Bill to enact the necessary legislation was introduced in November 1998, and passed in 1999; but already a limited number of local authorities are engaged in pilot projects to examine the practicalities of introducing Best Value into particular services, including a few planning authorities (Blackman 1998). Early in 2000, all local authorities will be subject to the Best Value regime. It will extend to all their functions, including their responsibility for town and country planning.

The government's intention is that Best Value will increase efficiency, effectiveness and economy, but will also facilitate the addressing of so-called 'cross-cutting' issues such as promoting sustainability and securing social inclusion. To what extent will central government's concern for social inclusion, particularly as filtered through Best Value, reorient planning authorities' concern? The next section begins by discussing what appears to be meant by Best Value and some of its conceptual and technical implications; it then reports on the degree to which local planning authorities are responding to the major change in prospect, drawing on preliminary results from a recent questionnaire survey of English and Welsh local authorities; finally, it considers the prospects for Best Value's being a way of increasing local planning authorities' sensitivity to promoting race equality.

What is 'Best Value'?

> Best value will be a duty to deliver services to clear standards – covering both cost and quality – by the most effective, economic and efficient means available...
> Best value is about doing the right things right.
>> 'Local Voices: Modernising Local Government in Wales',
>> CM4028, 1998, paras 7.2 and 7.7.

> the continuous search by a council to improve the quality, efficiency and effectiveness of all its activities for the public.
>> Geoffrey Filkin, quoted in Chelliah (1998: 1)

'Best Value' has the advantages and drawbacks of a memorable slogan. On the one hand, it is short, punchy and uses evocative terms, including a superlative with which no one can take issue as a target for any organisation; it could be described as inspirational, and is certainly a classic aspirational slogan. On the other hand, the term 'value' is notoriously contestable, one which continues to perplex philosophers and policy makers alike (Pattison 1998). Not surprisingly, then, 'Best Value' has been proving difficult to pin down (Centre for Public Services 1997).

One way to understand Best Value is simply to see it as a set of procedures, a process. So, we find in the July 1998 English and Welsh White Papers, *Modernising Local Government*, confirmation of a model first set out in a government consultation paper of a few months earlier, and summarised in a government memorandum to the Environment, Transport and Regional Affairs Committee (HM Government 1998: 87). Authorities responsible for achieving best value will be expected to demonstrate it by going through the following activities:

- a corporate approach to identifying areas of strength and weakness in service performance;
- a programme of fundamental performance reviews, systematically covering all areas of authority activity over a four to five year period: these reviews will challenge the purpose of the service(s) concerned and the way in which it is provided by other authorities and other providers; consult the local community on their aspirations and the balance between cost and quality; and require competition to ensure that, as far as possible, alternative sources of supply are thoroughly tested as to what they can deliver;[3]
- the setting of key performance targets covering efficiency, effectiveness and economy, and their publication in Local Performance Plans;
- independent audit/inspection of local authority performance, both annually and on completion of each fundamental performance review;

- in exceptional cases, where service failure has been serious and/or persistent, and where authorities have failed to take the necessary remedial action, intervention by Ministers to ensure improved performance.

(HM Government 1998: 87)

It is worth highlighting that authorities will set performance targets, and these will use a mixture of a relatively small number of national indicators and a large number of local performance indicators. Such an account begins to provide a picture of what Best Value might mean for local authorities, but it needs to be supplemented by a flavour of the ethos of the changes being promoted.

Best Value emphasises the corporate nature of local government and the requirement that it be responsive to the needs of the community, but it does not assume that local authorities are necessarily the best agencies to deliver services to meet those needs, nor that local authorities can be left entirely free to regulate themselves: standards must be defined and policed, by authorities *and* by external agencies.

Even such a schematic account of what Best Value involves confirms its potential for radically changing the face of local government. Unlike Conservative governments, which tried to whittle away the powers and prestige of local government, the Labour approach is to emphasise the local council's responsibility as an elected body, to devise and to promote a coherent and widely shared vision and set of priorities for its area (Blair 1998). Its duty is to ensure its objectives (and their translation into performance measures and standards) are subject to consultation and are widely agreed.

Moreover, the council must meet these objectives as efficiently, economically and effectively as possible. This may mean working with other organisations in the private and voluntary sector to provide services. In brief, the council is moving from an exclusively service delivery role to a strategic enabling role (Carter *et al.* 1991). If the spirit as well as the letter of Best Value is followed, then local authorities will be at the centre of complex, often overlapping, networks of individuals and various kinds of informal groups and organisations (who will include users, potential users and/or providers of services), engaged in regular dialogues about the objectives and quality of services, with the goal of achieving continual improvement. This is a very long way from the traditional service delivery model of local government.

Best Value and equal opportunities

Understanding the implications of Best Value for the promotion of equal opportunities is hindered by the ambiguity of both terms. Some of the complexity relating to Best Value has already been alluded to above. But as was pointed out in Chapter 1, equal opportunities is also open to different interpretations. Most significant of all, is the difference between a conception of promoting equal opportunities which views it as entirely a question of addressing potential (and actual) unfairness suffered by individuals, and an alternative which sees the key issue as a need to address collective or group injustice. A focus on the former approach will tend to emphasise fairness in relation to access to, or opportunities to enjoy, goods and services; it will prioritise the setting up of mechanisms for allowing individuals to seek redress for alleged unfairness when it actually occurs. The second approach, by way of contrast, will supplement the foregoing with a focus on the outcomes of processes, service delivery, recruitment and so on for general categories of people, categories identified (and defined) in accordance with a socio-political analysis of how the distribution of goods and services is, generally, skewed in favour of certain groups.

Put somewhat more specifically, the individualist conception of promoting equal opportunities in relation to 'race' will seek to eliminate prejudice and discrimination suffered by individuals in certain specified circumstances. While recognising that members of certain groups (black and ethnic minorities) are more likely to suffer such unfairness, the focus is on the fate of actual individuals who may (potentially) suffer, and the preferred actions are to set up procedures which ensure fairness of access/opportunity, and *post hoc* grievance procedures for individuals who feel unfairly treated. The sole focus is on specific procedures and processes. In the second, collectivist approach these procedures and processes are also of concern, but they are viewed as exemplifying much broader inequalities in social relations. On this view, a focus on procedures alone will always have limited (albeit real) success, as monitoring *outcomes* will demonstrate.

Returning to Best Value, we would argue that the Best Value regime creates the potential for a collectivist conception of equal opportunities to be pursued: 'where equal opportunities is a key corporate objective of a council, it will need to be addressed at every stage of best value' (LGBVP 1998: 4). But as we shall see, this is optional, and the government's own references to equal opportunities gesture at a thin version of the individualist conception. This may not only reflect the government's social philosophy but also the emphasis, in its discussions of Best Value, on process and procedure rather than content (Chelliah 1998; CPS 1997).

The implications of Best Value for promoting equal opportunities are actually less well-defined even than the notion itself, and in this they betray the long-standing marginal place of equal opportunities in local government (and indeed in local politics) (Ball and Solomos 1990). We have seen that the Commission for Racial Equality (CRE) has argued that 'equality means quality', and has identified a progression whereby local authorities can embed the promotion of equal opportunities increasingly deeply into their activities (CRE 1995). While a very useful document, it is of necessity quite general in relation to service delivery. We should not be surprised, then, that a 1997 review of the literature on Best Value found that 'there is little or no specific reference made to...equal opportunities and social justice' (CPS 1997: 5). Equity is noticeably absent from the 1998 Local Government Bill. The Bill's preamble, for example, states that it will: 'Make provision imposing on local and certain other authorities requirements relating to economy, efficiency and effectiveness...' The government's White Paper on Local Government refers to 'fair access' to services (7.14; 7.18), thus commending the individualistic conception of equal opportunities; but – as the recent LGBVP report on equalities and Best Value conceded – 'the White Paper does not explicitly make equality or equity a key principle of best value' (LGBVP 1998: 17). The report makes it clear that there are authorities which are considering in some detail how 'equalities' can be built into Best Value (see also Smith and Burgoyne 1998); but there is no clear picture of how widespread such interest is. Still less is there any overview of what is happening in relation to equal opportunities and Best Value in planning authorities.

There is no doubt that Best Value, is being taken seriously, at least in some quarters. There is a Best Value Group set up by the Planning Officers Society, DETR, RTPI, LGA, LGMB and Chartered British Institute of Public Finance Accountants (CIPFA). It intends to produce a Good Practice Guide in 2000, and thereby to influence the Audit Commission's 'diagnostic toolkit' for Best Value in Planning. The Planning Officers Society, meanwhile, has produced a report on performance indicators (POS 1997), while individual authorities have prepared internal reports on topics such as a 'Best Value Action Plan for Development Control' (Camden). In Wales – whose corporatist political culture allowed Best Value to be explored and promoted by central-local/CBI/TUC working party very early (Best Value Project Group, 1997) – local planning authorities appear to be networking extensively.

Equal opportunities in general, and race equality in particular, figure to varying extents in this flurry of activity. The Welsh Framework (BVPG 1997) makes no mention of equal opportunities, and has only a passing reference (on page 12) to improving the take up of services among 'target groups' (by improved marketing). Perhaps it is not surprising, therefore, that early indicators are that most pilot projects introducing Best Value in Wales are paying little or no attention to equal opportunities (though one is focusing on services for the visually impaired, the implications of which will be discussed below) (Boyne et al. 1999). The Planning Officers' Society (1997), on the other hand, specifically add equity as a fourth 'E' (to accompany the three Es of economy, efficiency and effectiveness) in their model of Best Value. In the context of a framework-setting paper they emphasise the significance of the distribution of outputs and the need for performance indicators relating to it. Given the continuing lack of interest of planning authorities in race equality in general (Krishnarayan and Thomas 1993;

Loftman and Beazley 1998a), it might seem wildly optimistic to expect this positive approach to have much impact on the ground. But there are two closely-related reasons for at least a degree of optimism in relation to Best Value and planning.

First, it is clear that the Best Value regime will apply to local authorities as corporate entities: each service will be expected to reflect the council's ethos, and contribute to meeting the council's objectives. To the extent that at least a flavour of the individualistic conception of equal opportunities – 'fair access' – is built into the way councils are evaluated, then each service will be expected to play its past in ensuring the council performs well on that measure. Of course, when councils adopt a stronger concern for equal opportunities as part of their corporate objectives then all services (including planning) will be expected to do that much more in relation to equal opportunities. Best Value does look set to sweep through local government, so planning authorities might be well advised to think about the implications of it for equal opportunities and their work.

The second reason for a justified expectation of some change in relation to race equality initiatives arises from the view that planning authorities – officers and members – respond to particular kinds of signals and pressures (see earlier discussion). Exhortation to do good deeds, in itself, is not enough; but a project defined in and backed by legislation, enjoying the evident approval of senior ministers (including the Prime Minister), and working (in some ways) with the grain of local authorities (inasmuch as it defines a key role for them in local governance) carries the message that it cannot be ignored, and that a sensible response is to work constructively for its implementation. As we have seen, there is scattered evidence that this is happening in local government.

Initial local planning authority responses to Best Value: a review and discussion

This section will present some of the results of a questionnaire survey of local planning authorities in England and Wales. As responses are still coming in at the time of writing, the paper will consider a subset, namely those from Welsh local planning authorities, where a response rate of 59 per cent (n=13) has already been achieved.[4]

It is clear that Best Value is by now a feature of the local authority landscape. In all respondent authorities there had been discussions of Best Value at senior officer levels within the council as a whole, and within the planning department. In just under two-thirds of authorities (eight of thirteen) there had been a council resolution to introduce Best Value into planning (typically as part of an authority-wide programme), and the same proportion also claimed to have an action plan for such implementation. We must bear in mind that Wales may exhibit an unusually high degree of interest in Best Value, as every unitary authority is engaged in piloting Best Value in at least one of its services. Not surprisingly, in these circumstances, twelve of the thirteen respondents reported their authority had a unit with corporate responsibility for Best Value, and a similar proportion said there was an inter-departmental team (usually consisting of senior officers meeting every two months or so, though sometimes including members also).

Though planning is only specifically included in pilot projects in three authorities, there is clearly a great deal of thinking about Best Value going on in other planning authorities too. Seven of the thirteen respondents (54 per cent) said they had identified 'stakeholders/users to be involved in defining the nature/objectives of the planning service'. They list these stakeholders in their own words, but most refer to applicants/agents and consultees, and the 'public at large' or 'the community'. A few mention councillors and planning staff. Two refer to existing consultative mechanisms (advisory committees, community council and so on). Only one disaggregates 'the community' and refers to 'business groups, farmers, unemployed, people with special needs'. Interestingly, these, it appears, are groups consulted as part of the department's Local Agenda 21 initiatives. Though it is very early days, it is not unreasonable to suggest that planning authorities will be tempted to define their service in terms of functions with very obvious users or beneficiaries (development control is the clearest case, but grant-giving might be another, and so on). Involving 'the public' may well be tackled via known representative organisations (Conservation Advisory Groups, for example) and/or sample surveys of the population. The danger here is conservatism; that the choice of stakeholders will be such as to broadly confirm the nature and objectives of the service. A little fine-tuning may be called for by such consultation, but probably little more.

This impression is confirmed by the responses on measuring economy, efficiency and effectiveness (the so-called '3 Es'). Sixty-two percent (eight) of authorities have decided how they will measure economy, and just over half have decided how they will measure efficiency and effectiveness. However, only one planning authority claimed to have involved stakeholders in defining appropriate measures, and only one other joined it in claiming to have involved stakeholders in discussions of how performance was to be assessed in relation to the measures (setting targets, for example). As there are so few replies, they can be listed in full (see display on page 104).

'The Community', it is true, is a term which can cover a great deal; it certainly offers scope for an explicit concern with equal opportunities. What appear to be the prospects for this? Ten of the twelve authorities responding to the question (83 per cent) claimed to have a departmental equal opportunities policy, and many went on to explain that this meant that their department subscribed to a corporate equal opportunities policy; one-third

Stakeholder re-appropriate measures:	councillors, community councils, 'key partners and agencies'.
Stakeholders re assessing performance:	LPA1: as above, plus service, users
	LPA2: Conservation Area Advisory Groups, Countryside Strategy Consultative Groups, City Centre Strategy Group, Community Organisations, 'The Community'

also claimed that there was an equal opportunities action plan for the planning department. However, the connection to Best Value does not seem to be being made.

Five authorities of twelve (42 per cent) claim to some aspect of introducing Best Value into their authority has involved a reference to promoting equal opportunities. Unfortunately, only two provide any supporting information: one refers to the future of the Welsh Language (a national planning objective), and the other refers to the way in which a corporate objective of 'minimising unfair disadvantage' has been translated into action and performance indicators for planning:

Action	Indicator
promoting equality of opportunity in the planning system reduce unfair disadvantage of any person, group, community through the planning system	monitoring of planning applications and decisions by ethnicity (1) level of satisfaction assessed by Access Committee for users
	(2) level of satisfaction assessed through segmentation analysis of all customer surveys

Four also claim that promoting race equality, specifically, has been a part of their moves to introducing Best Value, but the only evidence to support the claims is the ethnic monitoring noted above. It is also important to point out that in this local authority, whatever is claimed about 'stakeholder involvement', the reality is that the local Race Equality Council has had no contact with planners on any aspect of Best Value, and it is equal opportunities officers within the council who have ensured that equal opportunities has some place on the Best Value agenda. Overall, then, as with promoting race equality in planning more generally, the introduction of Best Value into planning seems to excite more interest about 'equalities' within national bodies than it does at local planning authority level. Yet, there are some reasons for being optimistic that over the next few years promoting equal opportunities may feature more fully as a feature of the planning service than it has hitherto.

First, the Best Value regime applies to every local authority service, and there is already guidance about how providing equal opportunities can be made a central feature of Best Value, and therefore apply to the planning service (see for example Figure 4.1). This means that a great deal of the discussion and argument which has dogged planning, for example about the very principle of ethnic monitoring, will be side-stepped (see for example Krishnarayan and Thomas 1993). Second, even this small sample turned up at least one example of how corporate objectives which have an 'equalities' dimension can be converted into local planning authority activities and targets. Exemplars of this kind can be extraordinarily influential when local authorities feel they are obliged to follow certain national policies. Finally, the Best Value approach is intended to open up reviews of services to groups and interests outside government. At present, local authorities seem to be taking a very conservative approach as to how stakeholders may be defined; this is understandable, if not wholly defensible, and needs to be challenged. At the moment, the potential of Best Value for opening discussions about services seems not to be widely appreciated outside local government, but if and when this changes, there should be institutional and political leverage available to force on to the agenda considerations about how planning contributes to overcoming racially-based disadvantage. On the other hand, as some commentators have already pointed out, if the current emphasis on process and procedure continues, questions of social justice and fairness will find no place in discussions of Best Value. At best, there will be scope for a thin, individualistic conception of equality of opportunity ('fair access' as opposed to 'fair outcome').

So far the discussion has considered planning as one local authority service among others. Because the literature on Best Value to date has tended to be written by local or central government officers there has been a tendency to look at its potential for improving services within broadly the same functional structure as at present. However, the Best Value approach can and should involve questioning that very structure from time to time, and this is especially important in relation to assessing the impact of government as a whole on disadvantaged groups. Perhaps the most exciting of the Welsh pilot projects relating to Best Value is that which focuses on a 'client' group – the visually impaired – and reviews local authority services from its standpoint. At present, the focus of the pilot seems to be services such as social services and education, and while one can understand why this might be, it is to be hoped that it goes on to consider planning policy (for example, how much time and effort should be devoted to securing a more accessible environment?). It is essential that the model of mainstreaming equality set

Mainstreaming Equalities into Best Value

| Proposed Best Value Performance Management Framework |

Consult about equality objectives and priorities with stakeholders

Establish authority-wide **corporate objectives** & performance measures

Ensure:
1 corporate objectives include explicit commitment to equalities and/or to objectives that benefit disadvantaged groups in the community
2 service objectives include their contribution to corporate equality objectives

Agree corporate **programme of fundamental performance reviews** and set out in local performance plan

Undertake fundamental **performance reviews** of selected areas of expenditure

1 Assess key service contributions to equality objectives
2 Identify ideas where service review needed to achieve/improve equalities
3 Input to corporate review & FPR programme

1 Challenge: how far is service provision meeting corporate objectives and local needs
2 Compare: service delivery and performance with other providers
3 Consult: investigate consumer, community, stake holder views
4 Compete: demonstrate that services are competitive

Consult with users:
Is the service accessible & appropriate?

Consult with non-users and under users

Set and publish performance and efficiency targets in **local performance plan**

1 Agree service/activity specific objective
2 Set improvement targets and local PIs
3 Monitor and report national and local PIs

1 Agree equality objectives as part of performance plans
2 Set equality targets and EPIs (in action plan)
3 Publish performance against equality objectives

Use outcomes to consult with stake holders and update corporate and service objectives and priorities

Independent **audit and inspection** and certification

Figure 4.1   Best value: incorporating the promotion of equal opportunities

Source: Local Government Best Value Partnership (1998)

out in Figure 4.1 is complemented by periodic reviews which consider the council (or governance networks more generally) as a whole from the perspective of particular groups. Only in this way will we be sure that Best Value begins to help deliver 'joined up local government'.

Conclusion

The struggle (or challenge) for me in writing this chapter has been to provide an accurate description of the planning system's engagement with the racial-isation of British society without generating an air of utter despondency. The brute fact is that there have been very few occasions on which any of the major players in the planning system – the politicians (local or national), professionals, or developers – have consciously taken account of racialisa-tion, or that which grows from it, racially based injustice. Consequently, there is a real danger that the planning system, by default, has tended to reinforce existing relations of power which are bound up with specific forms of racialisation (as discussed in Chapter 2). As John Forester has put it, 'Planners can expect the organisations with which they work not only to seek certain ends but also to reproduce, or refashion, social and political relations' (1989: 72).

The lack of research evidence about the effects of planning means that a definitive account of its impact on racialised minorities cannot be given. But the little evidence relating specifically to such minorities (such as data from monitoring) is not encouraging, and more general analyses of British plan-ning over the last twenty years portray it as tending to favour those who are already socially and economically privileged and successful; refashioning social and political relations in a progressive manner has not been a notable feature of planning practice (Healey *et al.* 1988; Brindley *et al.* 1996; Ambrose 1986; Allmendinger and Thomas 1998; Thornley 1993).

Dispiriting as these kinds of reflections can be, they need to be set against the possibility of progressive change. We can remind ourselves, for example, that there are policy areas where, in general, promoting equal opportunities is better established than it is in planning (as Moore (1995) pointed out); and there are planning authorities which have been at the forefront of their authorities' commitment to race equality (such as in Leicester). These exam-ples illustrate what is possible without any radical social change or a transformation of the planning system; so it is not utopian to work for change within planning, and complete despondency is not called for.

Working successfully for change depends upon having a good grasp of what is wanted, and why, and also on developing a strategy which is sensitive to political and professional realities. Much of this book relates to the former task, where it builds upon previous work by the CRE, RTPI and LGA. But it also tries to contribute to the latter task. Earlier in this chapter, for example, a simple model of factors influencing organisational change in local authorities was set out. Three factors were identified as especially significant for planning authorities: the national legal and political context, and local political and professional leadership. The former, it must be admitted, is difficult to influence, yet in relation to race equality and planning there are some positive factors to consider. First, there are at least two national organisations – RTPI and the LGA – which are committed to pressing for a higher priority to be assigned to race equality within government policy advice. This is important, as these organisations are regularly consulted by central government about planning. They provide an entrée, at least, to the central government policy-making machine. Second, whatever the uncertainties surrounding the government's understanding of 'social exclusion', the publicity surrounding the Macpherson Report has, for the moment, pushed race equality up the agendas of all government agencies. It may not last, but some important gains may be made while it does. Of course, this is only part of the complex of policy processes which constitutes planning, and in particular judicial interpretation of legislation in both planning and race relations has a track record of conservatism which is somewhat dispiriting (Lester 1998: McAuslan 1980). Yet there *is* scope for some change in the national context.

At local level, Krumholz and Forester (1990) have set out, albeit in a north American context, some of the opportunities which planners working for change may be able to exploit. They argue that the scope for influencing change arises from the following factors:

- The issues and problems planners are asked to tackle often need to be defined and shaped; in doing this, some concerns and values can be put at the foreground, others pushed to the background. (We have seen in relation to Best Value that precisely this kind of opportunity exists, but to date race equality has not, generally, been in the foreground).
- Planners have resources and abilities which others (bureaucrats, politicians, even business) need. My own experience is that planning departments or divisions are often among the most imaginative, lively (and yet also professional), in a local authority. They often engage in 'special projects' of various kinds. This gives them potential influence.

Of course, exploiting these opportunities depends upon an ability to network, politically and professionally. Moreover, as has been argued throughout, the influence of planners in policy processes other than technical ones may be extremely limited (though some are adept at involving themselves in local politics). Yet, the central point remains: working for change is not simply necessary, it also has some prospect of success. We will return to these themes in Chapter 6, having first discussed an aspect of the racialisation of British planning too often confined to the margins.

Notes

1   The titles of such posts vary between authorities, and over time. The terms of reference of the posts are often so vague, however, that titles such as 'race advisors' or 'ethic minority liaison officers' provide little guidance to their content. The discussion in this chapter draws heavily on Krishnarayan and Thomas (1993: 71).
2   A similar example is the black councillor who recounted how a fellow councillor once expressed surprise when she voted against the interests of a black person in a contentious planning matter.
3   Step 2 is often broken down into:

  • challenging whether policies and services are still relevant to the public, or whether others should take priority;
  • consulting on the form, quality and cost-effectiveness of services to meet the public's needs;
  • comparing performance with the best, both within and outside local government;
  • deciding the best way to procure services to compete with the best and preparing local performance plans.

   These are the four Cs at the heart of achieving Best Value.
4   An analysis of the full results will appear shortly in *Planning Practice and Research*.

Chapter 5

Gypsies, travellers and the planning system

Introduction

Virtually none of the major texts on race and planning in Britain say anything about gypsies. The RTPI's 1992 commissioned study excludes consideration of policies on gypsies (Krishnarayan and Thomas 1993), as does the report of the recent LGA survey (Loftman and Beazley 1998a); Thomas and Krishanrayan's (1994) collection of essays and case studies on race equality and planning, contains a chapter on 'The planner and the gypsy' (Home 1994), but this is an exception. I suspect that this silence is largely the result of a somewhat hazy perception of 'planning for gypsies' being a specialist subject with its own legal framework, case law and so on. In my own work on race equality and planning, I have also tended to shy away from thinking about gypsies and travellers. Writing this book has given me the chance to redress this, and in so doing to reflect on why policies in relation to gypsies and travellers are regarded as a specialist policy field. I believe that pre-theoretical intuitions that there are important differences are correct: gypsies and travellers are a racialised minority, but the manner in which this occurs differs markedly from other minorities because social relations with the rest of society are so different, based as they are on economic peripherality and nomadism. These latter factors introduce another complication inasmuch as there are now very visible groups of economically marginal nomads who are, typically, vilified, stigmatised and excluded from a wide range of social activities, but whose stigmatisation and exclusion is not justified by a racial ideology (these are the so-called 'New Age Travellers' – not a term they usually appreciate[1]). That gypsies and/or traditional travellers have been and continue to be the subject of racism is well-established; what is less clear is whether the racialisation of gypsies has changed because of the adoption of nomadism by groups who do not themselves claim any ethnic distinctiveness. Given these complexities, it seemed sensible to devote a chapter to gypsies and travellers, even though much of the thinking underlying earlier chapters (especially Chapter 2) drew upon writings such as those of Sibley (1981; 1995) which discussed gypsies, and, as will be seen, the general theoretical approach is the same as that deployed in the rest of the book.

This chapter will discuss the ways in which the planning system has treated, and had an impact upon, the lives of gypsies and travellers. It is pretty clear that the impact has been largely negative, particularly in England and Wales (see for example Home 1994; Morris 1998). Moreover, the evidence suggests that harsh treatment within the planning system makes a major contribution to a poorer quality of life in general for gypsies and travellers. For example, a number of studies of gypsies and travellers in England and Wales have concluded that their health and welfare was compromised by the disruption to their lives caused by uncertainty and harassment over stopping places (for example Davis *et al.* 1994; Hawes 1997). In Scotland, on the other hand, where a more positive approach has been taken to both the provision of sites and unauthorised encampment, a recent study of authorised and managed traveller sites found primary school attendance to be good and relations with local residents on the majority of sites to be good or very good (Douglas 1997: 19). The chapter's argument will be that the raw deal which gypsies and travellers have long experienced from the planning system should not only be viewed as a reflection of the lack of influence gypsies/travellers have in that system (which is itself an instance of a more general lack of political power). Of course it is that; but the experiences of gypsies and travellers are also important as a reminder of the role of planning in the (social) construction of discourses within which power is mobilised and exercised. So planning, it will be argued, has a role in constituting and upholding social relations of power and does not simply reflect them.

The chapter begins by briefly discussing what people might mean by the terms 'gypsies' and 'travellers'. It then reviews the ways in which gypsies and travellers have been relegated to the margins of academic and policy discussions, and the significance of racialisation in this process. The chapter goes on to discuss the ways in which the constructions of nation (and community more generally) have been racialised and the implications of this for town planning, which historically, and currently, is closely involved in creating visions which can unite and enthuse. In particular, it considers how gypsies and travellers might be excluded from the kinds of visions with which planners have been involved. One of the conclusions reached is that the notion of 'modernisation' has, in certain places and times, been a powerful component of visions designed to unite. Such a conclusion raises a query over the prospects for gypsies and travellers in the planning system of the new millennium, focused, as it seems to be, on promoting a New Labour agenda of modernising Britain. While it may just be possible to see how a modernising agenda can be compatible with (and might even embrace) combating the social exclusion of most racialised minorities, the nomadism and economic peripherality of gypsies and travellers seems guaranteed to ensure their continuing marginalisation.

Gypsies, travellers and public policy

Essentialist accounts of the 'true' nature or boundaries of ethnic or racial groups are, arguably, more prominent in discussion of gypsies and travellers than in the case of any other ethnic or racialised minority. Yet as Oakley (1997: 190) has argued, the ethnic boundaries of being a gypsy have been 'continuously created and recreated'. Nevertheless, not only have attempts been made to pin down gypsies through definitions in law and policy (see below), but also in everyday social practices as 'ordinary' people have tended to distinguish between 'real' gypsies and other groups, variously referred to as 'tinkers', 'travellers' or other terms (McKay 1997; Shuinear 1997). A recent review of development plans found fourteen which referred in their policies to 'bona fide Gypsies' (Wilson 1998: 20; see also Wilkin 1998: 109) while official counts of travellers have also drawn the distinction (Green 1991). Gypsies may not enjoy a high social status,[2] but – in these everyday discourses – they are at least afforded some kind of historically-based legitimacy as a genuine (and somewhat exotic) distinctive ethnic group; and in this respect, they are contrasted with other nomads who, it is suggested, are simply people who refuse to accept the conventions of the society into which they are born, yet are in some respect parasitic upon it (Davis 1997). Without accepting the prejudicial overtones of any proposed distinction, it does seem possible to distinguish (in broad terms) between new and traditional travellers, where 'the former term encompasses Gypsies, Irish Travellers and others with a long generational history of nomadism...[and]...possess a continuity rather than a community of culture', and the latter, admittedly 'less well-defined ...[is]... formed largely of young families with no generational history of travelling' (Hawes 1997: 9). Certainly, traveller politics makes this distinction, even if individual travellers or those who work with travellers may be less inclined to accept it (Acton 1997; Home 1994; Wilkin 1998).

The contrast between 'new and 'traditional' travellers is intended to acknowledge the adoption of a nomadic or semi-nomadic way of life from the 1960s onwards by 'hippies' or people 'dropping out'. However, as Davis (1997) points out, even as a summary of recent social history the distinction drawn is not quite as straightforward as it might seem, with the existence of an increasing number of second-generation new travellers, with some new travellers having a gypsy ancestry and, of course, traditional travellers themselves having recourse to a sedentary lifestyle for longer or shorter periods (Douglas 1997; Seabrook 1993: 172–83). More importantly, as with all social categorisations, the key question to ask is why is it being made and, more particularly, who is promoting or sustaining the distinction and to what purpose. In the case of gypsies and travellers, government and the courts have involved themselves in drawing distinctions between different kinds of travellers so as to identify those deserving particular governmental consideration. There have been legal references to gypsies in England and Wales for centuries, generally associated with their persecution (Fraser 1992). However, in recent times a legal definition of gypsy became necessary with the passing of the Caravan Sites Act 1968, which placed on County Councils, London boroughs, Metropolitan boroughs and county boroughs a duty to make sufficient site provision for gypsies who resided in or resorted to their area.[3] Central government grants were available for the development of sites, but by the early 1990s only 38 per cent of local authorities were designated as having sufficient sites for gypsies resorting to their area (Justice 1992).

Such a duty raised the question of entitlement to a site, and hence the need for a definition. Section 16 of the 1968 Act defined gypsies as:

> persons of nomadic habit of life, whatever their race or origin, but does not include members of an organised group of travelling showmen, or of persons engaged in travelling circuses, travelling together as such.
>
> (quoted in Home 1994: 113)

Wilson (1998: 2) has called this a 'non-ethnic' definition of a gypsy, and Home (1994: 113) argues that it, and the reasoning underlying it, has been instrumental in undermining attempts to have gypsies considered as a racial group under the Race Relations Act 1976 (though gypsies are now so considered; see Morris (1998)). However, a more recent court judgement appears to racialise the definition, by considering gypsies to be:

> persons who wandered or travelled for the purpose of making or seeking their livelihood, and did not include persons who moved from place to place without any connection between their movement and their means of livelihood.
>
> (Wilson 1998: 3, quoting Lord Justice Neil in *R* v *South Hams District Council ex parte* Gibb and two other applications)

Unsurprisingly, this definition was endorsed by a Conservative government in Department of Environment Circular 18/94 (Welsh Office Circular 76/94) Gypsy Sites Policy and Unauthorised Camping, and has recently been repeated in advice (Home Office/DETR 1998). The endorsement is unsurprising because the definition appears to be trying to distinguish between traditional travellers whose nomadic habits are wrapped up with a well-established ethnically distinctive way of life, and newer travellers who (by implication) simply travel on a whim, with no cultural or economic imperative to do so.[4] Something like this distinction was employed by some proponents of the Criminal Justice and Public Order Act (CJPOA) 1994. The CJPOA repealed those sections of the Caravan Sites Act 1968 which gave councils a duty to provide sites, and removed the Treasury's power to give grants to local authorities to cover the capital cost of building and maintaining gypsy sites. In addition, it introduced a number of criminal offences relating to trespass, the overall thrust of which was to give wide ranging police powers to remove trespassers and their property (including vehicles) from land and to inhibit (or prohibit) protests involving (or likely to involve) trespass; in Section 77, the Act criminalised all travellers without a secure pitch in England and Wales by making it:

> an offence for a person residing in a vehicle on any land forming part of a highway, or on any other unoccupied or occupied land without the consent of the occupier, to fail to leave the land as soon as practicable after receiving a direction from the local authority to move.
>
> (Clements and Campbell 1997: 66)

While the more extreme implications of the Act in relation to Travellers encampments have been blunted by judicial concerns (with respect to other legislation) for the welfare of children (Baber 1995), and subsequent advice has reinforced the message that basic welfare needs must be respected (Home Office/DETR 1998) it is nevertheless clear that the government had two major motives in promoting the legislation.

First, there was a desire to restrict the activities of a wide range of people deemed to be disruptive or anti-social. These included hunt saboteurs, anti-highways objectors and those attending raves, all groups which overlapped with the newer kinds of travellers (Clement and Campbell 1997). The second motivation was more directly related to gypsies, or traditional travellers, and was the belief that the provisions of the Caravan Sites Act put gypsies in 'a privileged position in terms of benefiting from public money' (Justice 1992: 5), and that they should assume the responsibility to provide sites for them-selves. (Of course, this demand ignored the fact that it is a series of social and economic changes – over centuries – managed and sometimes sponsored by the state, that has virtually destroyed the basis for the nomadic way of life in Britain (Sibley 1981)). Government Circular DoE 1/94, issued subsequent to the Act's being passed, anticipated an increase in planning applications for privately developed sites, though anecdotal evidence suggests this has not occurred. Both motivations thus stemmed from the government's desire to fashion a particular kind of Britain, and especially a certain kind of rural Britain, a country of settled, harmonious, self-reliant communities (Jess and Massey 1995). Within this vision, there is room for social diversity as long as it is ordered (Milbourne 1997), and arguably there may even be scope for a 'traditional' racialised 'other', but only on conditions which in practice are so onerous and unlikely to be fulfilled as to raise doubts about the sincerity of the desire to accommodate gypsies.[5]

Since the introduction of a comprehensive town and country planning system in Britain in 1947, gypsy sites have required planning permission.

When the development of sites was in effect a public sector activity, planning permission was simply part of the (sometimes anguished) political and professional discussion (and horse-trading) which accompanied site finding (see for example Sibley 1981). However, if more gypsy sites are to be privately developed, then the planning system should in principle guide such developments as it does any other kind of private sector development. In the plan-led system of the 1990s, this means that development plans should say something pertinent to a potential developer of a gypsy site.

Following the passing of the CJPOA, the Department of the Environment in conjunction with the Welsh Office issued two circulars relating to gypsy sites: DoE Circular 1/94 (Welsh Office 2/94), and DoE Circular 18/94 (Welsh Office 76/94). In relation to the location of gypsy sites, Circular 1/94 stated that henceforth gypsy sites should not normally be allowed in the Green Belt, a change of stance which could be presented as ensuring 'no special treatment' for gypsies, but also implicitly made the case that nomadism was to be accompanied by no different a relationship to the use of space than that afforded sedentary lifestyles. Moreover, green belts are intended to reinforce the definition of town and country, of the urban and rural (Murdoch and Marsden 1994), categories which have their contemporary material, emotional and ideological significance embedded in economic and social relations based on sedentary lifestyles.

The circular also anticipated that policies identifying either the locations of sites for gypsies and/or criteria by which to assess applications for such sites would be included in development plans (extremely important in improving chances of success for applications in the 'plan-led' system). A recent survey of the 403 English local planning authorities found that around 70 per cent had policies of some kind in their plans (this figure includes policies in draft and adopted development plans, because not all local planning authorities currently have an adopted post-1991 district wide plan (Wilson 1998)). Only two plans actually identified sites for gypsy caravans (1998: 7), and about a quarter of those which had policies, did not state the criteria against which planning applications would be judged (so-called non-criteria based policies, for example '...will allocate x number of pitches or sites in an area' (1998: 17)). Such policies give no guidance to an applicant for planning permission as to how to choose sites likely to be acceptable to an authority, and demonstrate in a particularly vivid way the potential of the plan-led system for excluding gypsies and travellers from areas. Some non-criteria based policies were found in strategic planning documents (Structure Plans, Unitary Development Plans (UDP) Part I), but only 54 per cent of the more detailed local plans and UDPs had criteria-based policies (Wilson 1998: 18).

Certain criteria emerge as being particularly common, and provide an indication of how local planning authorities view gypsies and travellers. The most common criterion (found in 71 per cent of criteria-based policies) is that a site be conveniently located for local services and facilities; and this concern that sites be functional is reflected too in criteria relating to vehicular access (58 per cent), capacity for servicing (47 per cent), and provision of parking (25 per cent) and play areas, storage and so on (15 per cent). A site must 'work', but it is also clear that, for many authorities, functionality is not enough; there is also a concern to minimise a perceived threat of conflict with sedentary residents. So 63 per cent of plans with criteria have one which seeks to avoid 'disturbance' or 'adverse impact' upon 'local residents/adjoining land uses' (Wilson 1998: 18); and 7 per cent actually state that a site shall not be within or close to a residential area. But perhaps more pervasive even than this concern, because it raises its head in so many subtly different ways, is the concern that the presence of gypsies and travellers not compromise the character of certain areas; that gypsies and travellers be kept in their place (see also Wilkin 1998). So 41 per cent of plans have criteria excluding them from protected areas such as Green Belts and Areas of Outstanding Natural Beauty (AONB); and an identical proportion have a criterion specifying that a site have 'no adverse impact on the environment/character and appearance of the countryside' (1998: 18). In 51 per cent of plans there are criteria requiring screening of a site or its 'assimilation' into its surroundings, and 6 per cent explicitly state that sites must be designed so as to prevent extension. (Reviewing public local inquiries in Scotland, Duncan (1995: 6) comments that 'inquiry proceedings sometimes appear obsessed with whether travellers sites might be visible to the general public'). It is clear that planning policies reinforce the construction of gypsies and travellers found more generally in public policy, as a threat to social order, as people 'out of place', and as best managed in spatially peripheral sites, typically screened from general view. In that respect, planning policy is only a particularly crude or blatant example of a more general strategy of state management of social tensions through spatial segregation (Pile *et al.* 1999).

As Wilson (1998: 12) points out, there is no evidence as yet of Circular 1/94, or development plan policies, leading to an increase in the provision of private sites for gypsies and travellers. Moreover, while in the 1980s opposition by local planning authorities to planning applications was to some extent offset by a relatively high success rate on appeal to the secretary of state (55 per cent in 1985), this rate appears to have been halved in the mid-1990s (Wilson 1998: 12), a consequence, we might surmise, of inspectors giving greater weight to development plans which are themselves unhelpful to gypsies and travellers wishing to develop private sites and a situation exacerbated by an apparent lack of will by local planning authorities to provide a suitable degree of advice and assistance to travellers and gypsies (Wilkins 1998). Meanwhile, Morris (1998: 640) argues that 'recent decisions...display powerful judicial reluctance to declare Gypsy policies unduly restrictive'.

In brief, then, the planning system (understanding the term to include a variety of policy processes) is an allocation of a resource which is vital to the traveller way of life: sites on which to live. Not only has the system not produced enough legitimate sites, but it also seems to perpetuate – in legal, professional and political discourses – distinctions between deserving and undeserving travellers which trade on intellectually discredited essentialist (and racialised) notions of ethnic difference.

The author's personal experience confirms the conclusions of the literature (for example Sibley 1981) that the consideration of gypsy sites is dominated by concerns about what councillors and/or 'the public' will accept. This attitude of quiescence and fatalism in the face of (anticipated) racism is also found in discussions of immigration, and often itself betokens a racial ideology which sustains a view that the racist attitudes are natural, even if reprehensible (Solomos 1989). An alternative approach is to accept that some people (proportionately, a tiny group) wish to be travellers. Their having sites on which to live is only one, albeit the most critical, of a number of ways in which they must interact with the rest of society. The planning process will therefore be an important but not the only arena within which understandings (and, perhaps, protocols) are developed which allow different ways of life in shared space. However, the starting point for this process, its base line, must be a recognition by the non-travelling population that travellers are not outsiders, visitors or 'Others', but are fellow-citizens; so that the task is not how to find ways of simply tolerating them, but to find ways of living with them, which will involve reflectiveness, openness and adjustments on all sides (Ravetz 1994).

Such a state of affairs will not arise simply through appealing to abstract notions of justice or fairness. Only political struggle will produce a better deal for gypsies and travellers; but it is important to recognise that this struggle must be along a broad front, for the manner in which gypsies and travellers are oppressed and discriminated against is complex. The occasions on which a planning committee votes *nem con* to refuse permission for sufficient stopping places for travellers in order to appease actual or anticipated popular protest is a dramatic manifestation of a complicated state of affairs. The immediate struggle may revolve around mobilising the support of councillors, doing deals or arguing about principles, as necessary (or expedient). But these dramas are embedded within ways of seeing (and understanding) the world, ways which are expressed in distinctive ways, in distinctive discourses.[6] In the next section, it will be argued that within some planning policy discourses gypsies and travellers can only be understood as marginal, even pathological, figures. Of course these understandings are not always unchallenged, but they are among the more influential of planning's contributions to understanding contemporary social life, and as such have not been helpful in bolstering the attempts to secure fairer treatment for gypsies and travellers in specific planning episodes.

Social cohesion, planning and gypsies/travellers

In this section, it is argued that a fruitful approach to explaining the nature of the planning system's interaction with gypsies and travellers can begin by considering the role of planning in promoting both images and the material reality of socially cohesive communities. It will begin by considering the nation (understood, following Anderson (1991), as an 'imagined community'). The argument seeks to establish two propositions. First, spatial form, which is influenced by planning policy, is important in both representing and helping to constitute social order (in particular, order presented as social unities such as communities or nations). Second, in the 1990s considerable political (and planning) effort has been invested in portraying places (counties, regions, cities) as modern, forward-looking places; this even extends to a particular reconstitution of rurality, which will be discussed. It will then be suggested that both newer and more traditional travellers sit uneasily in these visions of the modern town and country.

Penrose has argued that:

> the socio culture-political units which are commonly referred to as 'nations' are not immutable 'givens' but the produce of human thought and action. The existence of nations is not a truth that human beings have *discovered* but a conceptualisation of the world that we have *created*.
>
> (1993: 28)

Social construction of nationhood is not simply about defining who is inside and who is outside; it also incorporates what Moore (1994), speaking of the construction of gender, has termed 'fantasies of power', ideas about the appropriate power (and other) relations between members of one nation and another, and also, ideas about social relations (and relations of power) within the nation. Put briefly, the social construction of nationality is bound up in social relations of power which it can help undermine or reproduce. As constructions of gender and race also incorporate 'fantasies of power', as was discussed in Chapter 2, the construction of nationality will be gendered and racialised, and will be contested. And competing constructions of nationality will incorporate definitions of places which capture the essence of nationality (Gruffudd 1999).

The construction of nationality (or indeed, any other kind of social identity) will not be uncontested, and the precise nature in which it is undertaken will vary according to historical circumstances. Nevertheless Anthias and Yuval-Davis (1992: 26–7) have argued that there are certain interrelated elements in the idea of the nation constructed in the twentieth century which allow systematic discussion across a variety of circumstances. The nation of a common origin and a common history is potent, as is that of a common destiny, and the significance of either or both rests on the idea of there being a 'common solidarity' which binds people together. The emphasis placed on these elements will vary; in countries of immigration, for example, such as the USA, the idea of a common origin may be played down and that of a common destiny emphasised. However, there is nothing inevitable about this process; it is a product of political struggle. So in the UK, I would argue, the forward-looking aspect of the construction of nationality has been especially important in the media, in political discussion, in shaping public policy at certain times of social and economic upheaval since 1945, notably the immediate postwar period, the early and mid-1960s, and the middle and late 1990s. The 1951 Festival of Britain on London's South Bank, for example, 'was to be both a celebration of Britain's victory in the Second World War and a proclamation of its *national* recovery' (Conekin 1999: 228; emphasis added), and 'the reticent British were encouraged to proclaim confidence in their nation and their way of life' (1999: 234). But the Festival also tried to sketch a future for the country: 'The South Bank's architects and planners were…attempting to build a vision of a brighter future for Britain – a future that was clean, orderly and modern…' (Conekin 1999: 238).[7]

But such constructions have not been uncontested, and indeed, at other times of economic and social upheaval, an emphasis on *origins* has been more prominent in political and media discussions and has, as it were, set the pace (Solomos 1993). Currently, however, the emphasis is on the future, and particularly the future of Britain as a *modern* European nation. This, I will argue, has important implications for town planning.

Lewis (1998a) has argued persuasively that in defining its reach (that is, who should benefit and how), the post-1945 British Welfare State was also helping to define or construct the nation. It was, after all, a set of services promoted and supported politically as a material and symbolic consequence of a war in which all classes (and, more mutedly, all ages and both sexes) had shouldered burdens and contributed to the country's success. This task of constructing the nation was undertaken not only through national poli-cies and guidelines, but also in the day-to-day routines and procedures of state employees (of all kinds) throughout the country undertaking the kinds of taken for granted routines which O'Brien (1998) has argued sustain 'everyday inequalities' (often undermining official policies which try to counter discrimination). These local routines and procedures could, and did, vary but the evidence suggests that, in general, welfare services were contributing to a racialised construction of British nationality (Anthias and Yuval-Davis 1992). We saw in Chapter 3, for example, how in allocating council housing, housing services employed criteria which bore dispropor-tionately heavily on black and ethnic minorities thereby excluding them from the benefits of the service. Town planning was part of this racialised construction of 'who (really) belonged' in two ways. First, and perhaps most obviously, town planning assisted the delivery of some of the benefits of the state welfare programme: development of new housing areas, for example, and most spectacularly, the development of New Towns. As has been argued in Chapter 3, New Town development was implicated in the racial segregation of the postwar British population, while there is clear evidence of housing renewal policies, through their procedures and flow of benefits, reinforcing racialised social distinctions (Thomas 1999a). Such examples illustrate planning playing a role in defining or constructing the nation very much akin to other welfare services, helping to decide explicitly or implicitly who was entitled to benefit from its activities. The second way in which planning contributed (and continues to do so) to racialised nation-building was, however, quite different and has operated at the cultural level. This has been important in both forward-looking and backward-looking strands of constructing nationality.

Anthony King (1993) has argued that the development of the built environment simultaneously expresses and helps constitute a cultural order.[8] Writing of the spatial forms of the built environment, he points out that 'they not only represent a given social order, but in their physical, spatial and symbolic forms they actually participate in the construction of social and cultural existence' (King 1993: 263). The strength of this assertion needs to be underlined. Spatial form does not just reflect socio-cultural relations; it bolsters and helps reproduce them. This process is perhaps at its most obvious in debates and struggles over monumental development in major cities. Thus Jacobs (1996) analyses the 1980s arguments over the redevelopment of Mansion House Square in the City of London as, in part, struggles over differing conceptions of British nationality. One of these still valued the country's imperial past and the material it provided for constructing hierarchies of race and culture; the developers' proposals for redeveloping the site, on the other hand, emphasised modernity, interpreted as a break with history.

King uses the term 'spatial form', but actually focuses on the built environment; yet, in the construction of nationality, the nature of rurality and the relation of town and country can play their own significant roles. Allen *et al.* (1998) have argued that for thirty years or more the south-east of England has been a focus for competing constructions of rurality and simultaneously of Englishness. Newly affluent groups of people have sought to create a place in the country which is decidedly not 'traditional' (if that be read as 'moribund') but has a recognisable, usually visual continuity with the elitist, traditional, land-owning culture which has created and dominated that space for centuries. As Murdoch and Marsden (1994) show, this process involved shaping a particular kind of place and simultaneously defining who belonged in it, thereby shaping class relations and those of gender and race. For our purposes, what is interesting is that new places are 'white' places and they are modern places (Allen *et al.* 1998), and again, these terms are jointly defined: 'whiteness' is socially constructed here and can be inflected to accommodate occupation/class position, so that the occasional Asian hospital consultant is acceptable as a neighbour (on the one hand), but young Asians, who might be deemed quintessentially modern, are careful about which leisure spaces they use and are often happier going to London for recreation (Watt 1998). Planning policies – in particular, those which restrict urban growth (such as green belts), and define appropriate uses for rural areas – have been vital tools in the task of translating contested ideals of rurality (typically nostalgic) into material reality (Murdoch and Marsden 1994). Proposals for new settlements may be opposed on the grounds that they threaten to destroy or compromise landscapes integral to a particular way of portraying, and understanding, ways of life deemed to be at the heart of the nation. In areas of heavy development pressure, which is what we have been discussing, they may well be branded as the 'thin end of the wedge', a step on a slippery slope; but whether this is the whole story is more debatable, as the Bhaktivedanta Manor case, mentioned in Chapter 2, illustrates. But even where development pressures are not so great – as in rural West Wales, for example – long running opposition to a generally well-regulated settlement with a revolving population of 'new' travellers, in so-called Tipi Valley, is plausibly explained as concern over the threat to a particular Welsh rural way of life, a conception which again is racialised (Evans 1995; Williams 1995).

These examples have emphasised the role of planning in valorising tradition, origins and 'the soil', but town planning has also been important in helping culturally encode (Jackson 1989) the urban (and rural) environments as appropriate for a nation with a future, as places for people sharing a common destiny, as places of social progress. In the immediate postwar period, this was especially evident: the *New* Jerusalem was to be material reality, and high profile initiatives such as New Towns were tangible illustrations of a people pulling together as they moved into the future. There was a similar emphasis on planning in the middle and late 1960s, as the policy makers anticipated explosive demographic and economic growth (Ward 1994); and in the 1990s town planning is decidedly part of the Blairite modernising agenda being required to reconsider its purpose and methods (DETR 1999) and, significantly, being expected to help deliver places appropriate for the new kind of Britain. The Urban Task Force's (1999a: 4) statement of its vision begins: 'As a nation, we will prioritise the development of our towns and cities by...'. It continues:

> The Task Force's remit is primarily a physical one, about buildings and spaces, but our vision has to extend well beyond bricks and mortar. It must be inclusive in its scope.

It desires

neighbourhoods that are well connected to each other and to urban centres, where social contact is encouraged...

The argument to date has focused on the construction of nationality, but analogous arguments can be devised in relation to other examples of the social construction of social unity; for example, the construction of urban community/civic unity. The corollary is that the critique of planning and public policy applies also across spatial scales. For example, there is a tension between the Urban Task Force's invocation of the nation and its concern for inclusivity. The boundaries of the nation include and exclude; it is the argument of this chapter that the current nature, and the history, of relations between gypsies and travellers and the sedentary population make it extremely unlikely that gypsies and travellers can be accommodated in contemporary constructions of social unity, whether it involves nations, or communities more generally.

This is because of the current emphasis on the linked notions of modernity and progress. The content of these ideas is itself, of course, a site of struggle, and one must not underestimate the number of uses which are largely emotive and devoid of much content. However, what seems clear from case studies of city boosterism (for example, Thomas and Imrie 1999) and analyses of the New Labour public policy discourse associated with notions such as 'exclusion', 'citizenship' and 'stakeholding', which are part of the modernising agenda (for example, Levitas 1998), is that a key component of 'the modern' community is economic integration and, by implication, an accompanying social discipline. Public policy, including planning policy, is often particularly concerned about creating the appropriate symbols of a modern town, region or country, and thus with the presence of certain kinds of economic activity (such as 'high-tech' firms, although the 'flavour of the month' changes pretty regularly) and certain kinds of architecture (Zukin 1991).

This notion of the modern revolves around a polarity between centrality and peripheralisation, sometimes expressed as integration and marginalisation. The modern town or region is one which is integrated and non-peripheral (though the criteria by which centralisation/peripherality are to be judged are contestable: Merseyside is, one presumes, central in the worldwide network of Beatles' fans, but is deemed peripheral in European regional development. If global space is best understood as constructed through dynamic social networks (Massey et al. 1999), then peripherality will be relative to a given set of social relations. The argument of this section is that contemporary town planning is supportive of particular constructions of space, in which a particular construal of 'the modern' is important and in which nomadic ways of life will be deemed peripheral.) In this respect, gypsies differ from other racialised minorities, whose aspirations and conception of the good life are not inconsistent with the vision of a modern Britain (or a modern city within it) sketched out above. It is with such minorities in mind that the Institute for Public Policy Research, for example, has called for a 'rebranding' of Britain as multi-cultural (Dodd 1999).

But both materially and symbolically – that is, in their day-to-day routines and the ways in which they sustain themselves, and the popular images of them, developed over centuries, and rarely challenged politically – gypsies and travellers are incompatible with a currently dominant conception of the modern. While gypsies and travellers have shown a remarkable degree of economic flexibility and adaptability over many years (Sibley 1981), their lack of formal education and a desire to retain economic independence (Sibley 1998) means that their work is unlikely to be convincingly portrayed as 'cutting-edge'. Going further than this, some have argued that nomadism marks out gypsies in the eyes of the sedentary population as subversive. Nor do their sites and pitches satisfy the kinds of aesthetic criteria demanded of the modern. In a word, gypsies and travellers do not fit into a planning ethos which values this particular conception of progress, of the modern. In itself this might not matter, were it not for the fact that this conception has been for some time an important element in constructing ideas of social unity. Gypsies and travellers fall outside of these constructions more certainly than other racialised minorities.

It might be plausible then, to see anti-nomadism as the key component in the harassment of, and hostility to, both newer and more traditional travellers. However, I think this view is mistaken; or, at least, it is if it considers nomadism simply as travelling from place to place, with no permanent settlement (a characteristic, it should be noted, of some financial 'high flyers' (Allen 1999)). The 'Otherness' of travellers, old and new, is constructed around the nature of their social relations, interpreted broadly, and their evident unwillingness to change them. It is not their moving from place to place that is at issue; this movement simply underlines the nature of (or lack of) their relations with a range of powerful institutions (schools, banks, the parish church or local mosque, and so on) Many of us will know 'pillars of the community' who are resident in any one place for less time than many a traveller, but their travels are part of their jobs as television executives or whatever. They travel but remain integrated, via bank accounts, mortgages, salaried employment and a myriad other relations. They may not be ideal members of a neighbourhood watch scheme, but they are never candidates for being outsiders in urban society (Sibley 1981). The racialisation of gypsies/travellers is one historically contingent inflection of an exclusion which the group currently shares with others. It is no more acceptable for that, and historically has had catastrophic consequences for gypsies themselves. Moreover, planning policies which help reproduce a socio-spatial order which excludes travellers in general are doing nothing to help address the racialisation of some of their number.

Notes

1   Davis *et al.* (n.d.) point out, on the basis of their research in south-west England, that travellers generally disliked the term 'New Age Traveller', preferring the term 'traveller' (if a label had to be used at all).

2   Hawes (1997: 5) refers to a survey which claims (of gypsies and travellers) that 'it can be shown that they experience, in their daily lives, the most extreme prejudice and discrimination of any minority to be found anywhere'.

3   The law in Scotland and Northern Ireland in relation to gypsy sites differs from that in England and Wales, but the issues of the racialisation of travellers, and discrimination against nomads are also live ones in Scotland and Ireland (see for example Noonan 1998).

4   It is the implicit suggestion that there is some essential link between nomadism and economic activity which defines a gypsy by, as it were, governing his or her life in some primitive way that marks this out as a racialised definition.

5   Wilkin (1998) argues that planning authorities in rural areas are more likely than urban authorities to distinguish between traditional and non-traditional travellers because the distinction is one which has resonance in rural areas. But she also argues that whatever distinctions are drawn, there is no significant general difference in the treatment of travellers of any kind by the two kinds of authority.

6   The term 'discourse' is one with a myriad of precise and less precise meanings. In this context, I am following McDowell's (1994: 162) approach that 'simply defined, a discourse is a way of thinking or writing about a subject. It produces meaningful knowledge within a system of thought or a set of codified knowledge. All statements operate within a particular discourse, which defines or limits how we think about things'.

7   Commentators disagree on the significance of the futuristic and backward-looking referents of the Festival (Conekin 1999: 228). It seems clear to me that the former predominated, but for reasons discussed earlier in this section we might expect any festival concerned with bolstering nationhood to also allow a nostalgic reading.

8   'Culture', another complex idea, in this context means: 'A set of ideas, customs and beliefs that shape people's actions and their production of material artefacts, including the landscape and built environment. Culture is socially defined and socially determined. Cultural ideas are expressed in the lives of social groups who articulate, express and challenge these sets of ideas and values, which are themselves temporally and spatially specific' (McDowell 1994: 148).

Chapter 6

Concluding comments

This book has discussed the implications for planning of its operating in a particular racialised society, namely Britain. Its primary purpose has been to suggest an analytical approach to understanding contemporary processes of the racialisation of social relations, because this is the essential basis for a planning practice which promotes race equality. For example, a sound analytical base highlights the danger that public policy (including planning policy) may serve to reinforce ethnic or racial categories which are socially constructed and embody inequalities of power and influence. To be sure, we need policies which seek to redress injustice based on racialised categories, but these must be supplemented by policies which try to undermine the categories, to dissolve them or drain them of social significance. Otherwise we run the risk of characterising public policy as simply a curb on natural or primeval antipathies between procrustean racial or ethnic groups. The promotion of equal opportunities – defined in either the liberal or radical senses discussed in Chapter 1 – should have, at its core, a tension between redressing immediate grievances and injustices and realising that doing so involves using categories which it is necessary to undermine, in the medium and longer term. The ethnic or racial categories used in monitoring exercises, for example, must not be allowed to give credence to racial ideologies, for all that they are essential to generating data on the distribution of the costs and benefits of policies and practices (see Chapter 2).

This book is not intended to be a manual for pursuing race equality in planning, but it is reasonable for readers to expect some discussion of the implications of its approach for planning practice. This chapter will provide this, setting its discussion within a review of two current debates of especial importance to planning in a racialised Britain. One is a debate about the future of urban life, with particular reference to two key reports – the Macpherson Report (1999a, 1999b) and the report of the government's Urban Task Force (1999b). Both reports try to set out a positive future for urban life, but – curiously, in an era of joined-up government – their analyses do not mesh. The other area of discussion is the future of Britain in Europe, which has implications for the planning system (Nadin 1999) and for the politics of race. Some of the key elements of the latter will be reviewed, in effect providing an update of Chapter 3. These ruminations, beginning with those on Europe, are found in the next section of this concluding chapter; an approach to promoting race equality in planning follows as the chapter's (and book's) final section.

Urban life in Britain: current policy debates and prospects

For good or ill, the creation of the European Union, as it is now styled, has been one of the great political projects of the twentieth century. What part Britain should play in the project has been one of the major fault lines in the country's politics for decades. For those engaged in creating an ever more effective Union, as much as for those opposing it (in Britain and elsewhere), the question of what it means to be European is central. Proponents of the 'European project' have needed and will continue to need to construct and promote a European identity which is attractive across national and regional boundaries, and does not obviously cut across or devalue national or regional identities. Many of those opposed to the European project argue that the creation of a stronger European identity can only be at the *expense* of national identities; that is, in terms reminiscent of the cultural racism discussed in Chapter 2, they regard a national identity and a European identity as mutually exclusive. Clearly, the issue of what constitutes European identity is a live one; and just as in the case of national identity (see Chapter 5), the construction of such an identity is contested and is not simply a matter of words or formulae in documents. European identities are constructed in social practices, for example in decisions on immigration and settlement within the union, in educational exchanges, and in dealings with peoples taken as constituting a non-European 'Other'. This is not to suggest that, at present, the construction of a European identity is central to racial formation and racism in Europe.[1] But the struggle over European identities will be an important part of the terrain in which anti-racist struggles will be conducted. The consequences of these struggles are difficult to predict: for example, what might be the effect of relatively successful struggles to create and sustain a non-racialised European identity on national identities which may be racialised? For the moment, however, such speculations are certainly idle, because the constructions of being European which are bandied about in the media, and in politics, seem to draw distinctions between Europe and 'the rest' which trade on contrasts between civilisation and barbarity which have considerable historical resonance (Hall 1992). For example, in the early days of the 1999 NATO war against Serbia, the BBC reporters sought to underline the horror of the plight of Kosovan refugees by emphasising that the scenes from the makeshift refugee camps were from Europe (by implication, not from some barbarous part of the world such as Africa, where such sights are commonplace).[2] The countries of the European Union grow ever more concerned, and stone-faced, about immigration (Gabriel 1994). The British experience is that the politics of immigration is swiftly racialised, and it is difficult to see how this can be avoided in Europe as a whole: in countries where racial discrimination already affects certain groups, how can controlling the entry of people who share some key (racialised) characteristics *not* have repercussions in domestic politics?

Planners can no more insulate themselves from the politics of race in Europe than they can in Britain. This needs underlining because influential voices among professionals and academics have been very positive about 'Europe', either in the sense of thinking British planning can learn from Europe, or (alternatively) embracing the opportunities offered by membership of the EU to undertake planning in a certain way. Under the former heading could be classed arguments in favour of creating livelier 'twenty-four hour' cities, with vibrant public spaces and cafe society; all, we are told, characteristics of European cities.

An example of seeing Europe (or more specifically, the EU) as an opportunity for positive planning might be lobbying for Objective 1, or for some other favoured status, within the EU's regional development strategy. Another example would be the way in which a county like Kent has established strategic planning links with the Pas de Calais, and the rather more modest (but extensive) networking undertaken by towns and cities up and down Britain. The recent (summer 1999) report of the Urban Task Force (1999b), hailed as 'one of the key points in the history of urban policy' (MacDonald 1999: 5), has also drawn on the experience of European cities. The 300-page report brings a wealth of research findings and practical experience to bear on two key questions: how to improve the quality of urban life in Britain, and how to accommodate a high proportion of the new dwellings which are likely to be needed in the next ten to fifteen years (Rogers 1999). These questions are linked, certainly in the mind of the Task Force's chairman, and (one presumes) in the minds of the politicians who commissioned the report. Putting the matter very crudely, the overarching question is how do we make urban life attractive for those who have some choice over where they live ('choice' here, being defined in terms of an effective presence in the market). This question itself begs a number of others. In particular, it skates over the way in which government action structures the housing market (or, perhaps, it is simply that the objective is to relieve as much development pressure on greenfield sites as is possible, so that government action in pursuit of sustainability can remain low-key and low-profile).

In any event, the focus of the report is creating cities which are attractive to a particular set of people. The Task Force would argue that a town or city which is attractive for one set of people will be attractive for all: for example, the positive externalities from creating a well-designed public realm will benefit everyone. This is one of the reasons for its advocating socially mixed

neighbourhoods (Urban Task Force 1999b: 65). Perhaps so, but the significance of such benefits may vary considerably and systematically according
to one's circumstances. On page 140 there is a pen-portrait of changes in
Schilderswick, the 'poorest district of The Hague'. Here, the public realm
has been improved, and 'coherence' has been brought to the 'urban texture'
as part of an urban regeneration programme stretching over twenty years.
Yet, the area has an unemployment rate of 41 per cent, an average annual
income per head 60 per cent of the city's average, and 80 per cent of the residents are 'of foreign descent'. The Task Force feels able to conclude that:
'The efforts of the Hague demonstrate that physical renewal is an essential
part of the urban solution but it will never be all the solution' (page 140).
Wisely, perhaps, they do not estimate just what proportion of a solution it
represents in somewhere like Schilderswick.

Of special interest to the theme of this book, the Task Force makes virtually nothing of the racialised segregation which appears to blight The
Hague, and which is part of a wider pattern of racial discrimination in
Britain. On page 45 it states that 'at the heart of our vision for a culturally
diverse and socially equitable city is a commitment to positive community
relations and ethnic diversity'; for 'discrimination against and exclusion of
different communities – in particular ethnic and other minorities – will
undermine the sustainable city'. The 'serious marginalisation which many
ethnic communities actually face' (page 45) should not be glossed over, it
states. Yet, the report says nothing about tackling racism and racial discrimination. Like the government commissioned evaluation of urban policy in
England to which it refers (Robson *et al.* 1994), it talks (for example in
Chapter 5) of partnerships, of community involvement, of making connections and creating coalitions; but not of the way all these processes can be –
and in the context of contemporary Britain are likely to be – racialised.

The city which the Urban Task Force hopes to shape is light years away
from that described in another landmark report of 1999, the Macpherson
Report on the police inquiry into the murder of Stephen Lawrence. Through
the cool, measured tones of an official report emerges the outlines of
contemporary city life for very many people, a life heavily influenced by
racism (either as victims or resistors, or as perpetrators, or indeed, simply as
residents of areas where it is a fact of life, part of the daily grind). At its
most frightening, racism is bound up with a violent sub-culture on dead-end
estates; but the report makes it plain that it believes racist 'canteen cultures'
are not the sole preserve of the police, and that institutional discrimination
(defined in Chapter 1 of this book) pervades British life, and not only urban
life. It is the significance of this pervasiveness – analysed in this book –
which the Task Force fails to appreciate. Its rather piously expressed aspirations for an inclusive society are not buttressed by an analysis of what
racism and racial discrimination are, nor of what may sustain them. They
ignore the lessons of decades of practice in fields such as housing (see

Chapter 3), and consequently ignore the possibility that the delivery of urban regeneration, to take one example, may be undertaken in a way which systematically disadvantages racialised minorities.

What does it mean to take this possibility into account? The next section provides some pointers for practice.

Race equality and planning: pointers for practice

A central message of this book is that those promoting race equality within, and through the workings of, the planning system need to understand the ways in which planning – both as a social practice itself, and through influencing social and economic processes – plays a role in the social construction of race(s) and the racialised distribution of social 'goods' and costs. Drawing on work related to gender equality (Braithwaite 1998; Verloo 1994), the few paragraphs which follow explore some of the implications of this perspective on race and planning for developing a more progressive practice.

As already noted, analysis is fundamental, an analysis which is sensitive not only to what Braithwaite (1998: 23) calls 'practical needs', but also to 'strategic needs': that is, not only needs related to socially accepted (and constructed) roles, but also ones which address imbalances of power which shape, and are sustained by, those socially constructed roles. The schematic analysis presented in Chapter 2 argued that the material basis for the social construction of social identities/categories (including races) lay in three spheres, the economy, civil society and the state, and in their interaction. Moreover, it argued that the nature and outcome of struggles in these spheres, and their interaction, were historically and spatially contingent. What we have, then, are broad guidelines about how to begin to analyse race formation in a given locality. If we follow Warde (1988), the key processes are the workplace regime, the nature of the local labour market and the reproduction of labour power. The state, at local and extra-local levels, will be involved in each of these activities and the planning function will play its role. For example, planning may foster an 'urban renaissance' which has huge implications for the nature of civil society – how people bring up their children, associate with each other, spend their leisure and so on – as well as implications for urban labour markets (the kinds of jobs available in cities; the kinds of people living near to those jobs; and, of course, planning organisations are themselves active as buyers in the labour market). And, as argued in Chapter 2, these processes will not only be implicated in racial formation but also simultaneously in class and gender formation (as well as relations between generations).

This sounds complex, and a fully researched analysis *will* be complex; but, of course, we do not begin as complete outsiders in any locale. There will be existing evidence and experience of racialisation and racial discrimination in an area. This may only be a starting point for analysis, but it will be a significant one. So, for example, in Cardiff successive surveys and censuses have shown quite marked residential segregation by ethnicity or birthplace, and moreover, areas with proportions of non-white residents and local images of being 'black' areas (even where there have been three or four generations of black residence) remain among the most deprived parts of the city. These data – which we can loosely refer to as outcomes of monitoring – point to a need to examine more closely the way housing is allocated in Cardiff, both through the market and the social housing sector, to see if (and how) racialised categories play a part. This can be difficult work, and I am not suggesting that complete sociological analyses of an area are necessary before any action on race equality is contemplated. How much analysis is needed at any time is something to be determined and argued over in specific circumstances. But understanding *is* needed; moreover, as Braithwaite (1998: 13–28) points out, broad involvement in undertaking that analysis is essential. In our case, racialised, gendered and other minorities have both knowledge of, and an obvious stake in, the processes being analysed (and, of course, critically reflective members of the racialised majority have much to contribute as well).

A degree of analysis is vital, for it will enable policy formulation to be better informed in relation to what needs addressing and how specific policies or projects will help address those needs. If the analysis has engaged a broad range of interests, then continued involvement in policy formulation may be desirable. However, these are issues which can only be definitively addressed in concrete circumstances. Whatever the local specificities, however, the broad areas with which any race equality strategy must concern itself (following the analysis of Chapter 2) are: employment and training; housing and welfare; and citizenship and political rights and influence (Allen 1999).

I can well imagine that the reaction of many planners and local councillors will be, 'we can't go in for academic studies of race formation and racism'. I cannot argue in the abstract about their priorities, but I do hope to have provided a context within which the actions of planners and others can be evaluated, however much or little they wish or are able to do. So, for example, if the introduction of the ethnic monitoring of planning applicants is considered, not only will the practicalities of getting any system to work be discussed (on which there is plenty of advice; see for example Riley 1994), but there will also be an awareness that ethnic and racial categories are socially constructed. So there are no absolute 'right' or 'wrong' categories. Consequently, planning authorities will need to ask themselves what categories are most relevant to meeting their purposes in undertaking monitoring. For example, if there is a suggestion that some local peculiarity of racial formation is exercising an influence over the planning process (such as the racialisation of a particular immigrant group, like the Irish; or a refugee community, such as the Somalis) then, with due discussion of its significance with affected parties, there may be value in identifying this group on the ethnic monitoring form. But all those involved also need to be sensitive to the way in which exercises such as monitoring can help construct such categories, and this effect must be weighed up against the benefits derived from acquiring systematically collected data.

Those involved in planning, in whatever capacity, have had a wealth of practical advice on how to begin to address issues of race equality (RTPI/CRE 1983; CRE 1995; Gilroy 1993; Krishnarayan and Thomas 1993; Loftman and Beazley 1998a; Chapter 4 above). The final passage in the book will try to distil a few general messages or maxims which should be borne in mind, in the light of the analysis of earlier chapters.

- There is widespread racialisation of British life, though constructions of specific racial categories may not share a common cause and may vary over space and time; racialisation is the ideological and practical under-pinning of racial discrimination.
- Racialisation is a socio-spatial process; inasmuch as planning involves managing space it will play its part in the racialisation of social relations; conversely it has an important role to play in promoting race equality.
- Given the extent of racial discrimination in British life, and the way it has been shown to influence activities from housing to sport to law enforcement it must be assumed that discrimination, or injustice of some kind, occurs in planning (though this need not mean that the rele-vant legislation is always infringed); the planning system must monitor its processes (and outputs) to ensure that discrimination is identified, and addressed.
- The complexity of the planning system – with its intertwined policy processes – means that careful, systematic analysis and plans of action are needed by all those involved in securing greater race equality through planning, and within planning.

Notes

1   There is widespread acknowledgement that 'Everywhere in Europe, racism seems to be on the increase' (Miles 1994: 198; see also Solomos and Wrench 1993; Khakee *et al.* 1999), but there is less consensus about the extent to which factors operating at a European scale are responsible for this phenomenon (Rattansi and Westwood 1994; Wrench and Solomos 1993). However, Gabriel (1994: 156) has suggested that 'in global terms the construction of common European cultural identity is, arguably, as significant as – possibly more than – the sum of Europe's national chauvinisms'.

2   At other times, in other places, it must be said, the boundaries of 'Europe' are constructed discursively in a much tighter way: films like *Midnight Express* portray Turkish people as an oriental 'Other', and the Balkans, it is often implied, is an extension of this Orient, with its primitive blood-lust, rather than an outpost of Europe (Glenny 1999).

Bibliography

Abram, S. *et al.* (1996) *The Social Construction of 'Middle England': The Politics of Participation in Forward Planning*, Cardiff: Department of City and Regional Planning, Cardiff University.

Acton, T. (ed.) (1997) *Gypsy Politics and Traveller Identity*, Hatfield: University of Hertfordshire Press.

Ahmad, W., Darr, A., Jones, L. and Nisar, G. (1998) *Deafness and Ethnicity*, Bristol: Policy Press.

Ahmed, Y. and Booth, C. (1994) 'Race and planning in Sheffield', in H. Thomas and V. Krishnarayan (eds), *Race, Equality and Planning: Policies and Procedures*, Aldershot: Ashgate.

Aldridge, M. (1979) *The British New Towns*, London: Routledge and Kegan Paul.

Allen, J. (1999) 'Cities of power and influence: settled formations', in J. Allen *et al.* (eds), *Unsettling Cities*, London: Routledge.

Allen, J., Massey, D. and Cochrane, A. (1998) *Re-thinking the Region*, London: Routledge.

Allmendinger, P. and Thomas, H. (eds) (1998) *Urban Planning and the British New Right*, London: Routledge.

Alty, R. and Darke, R. (1987) 'A city centre for people: involving the community in planning Sheffield's city centre', *Planning Practice and Research* 3: 7–12.

Ambrose, P. (1986) *Whatever Happened to Planning?*, London: Methuen.

Amin, K. and Oppenheim, C. (1992) *Poverty in Black and White*, London: Child Poverty Action Group.

Anderson, B. (1991) *Imagined Communities*, 2nd edn, London: Verso.

Anon. (1984) 'Outcry over the skyrail scheme', *South Wales Echo*, 11 April.

Anthias, F. (1992) 'Connecting "race" and ethnic phenomena', *Sociology* 26: 421–38.

Anthias, F. and Yuval-Davis, N. (1992) *Racialised Boundaries*, London: Routledge.

Appadurai, A. (1999) 'Dead certainty: ethnic violence in the era of globalization', in B. Meyer and P. Gescheire (eds) *Globalization and Identity: Dialectics of Flow and Closure*, Oxford: Blackwell, 305–24.

Armstrong, H. (1997) 'Keynote address', in *Proceedings of 'Best Value: How Does Value for Money Become Best Value?'*, London: Capita.

Ashcroft, P. (1992) 'Ethnic minorities and the environment: why the fuss?', in *Conference Proceedings: Ethnic Minorities and the Environment*, Sheffield.

Association of London Borough Planning Officers (ALBPO) (1998) *Quality of Outcome Practice Note No. 1 (First Draft)*, London: ALBPO.

Atkinson, R. and Moon, G. (1994) *Urban Policy in Britain*, London: Macmillan.

Audit Commission (1993) *Putting Quality on the Map: Measuring and Appraising Quality in the Public Service*, London: HMSO.

Baber, P. (1995) 'Wealden set to fight quashing of New Age travellers eviction', *Planning Week*, 7 September, 5.

Bagguley, P. *et al.* (1990) *Restructuring: Place, Class and Gender*, London: Sage.

Ball, H. (1988) 'The limits of influence: ethnic minorities and the Partnership Programme', *New Community* 15(1): 7–22.

Ball, W. and Solomos, J. (eds) (1990) *Race and Local Politics,* London: Macmillan.

Bariot, R., Bradley, H. and Fentson, S. (1999) 'Re-thinking ethnicity and gender', in R. Bariot, H. Bradley and S. Fenton (eds) *Ethnicity, Gender and Social Change,* London: Macmillan, 1–25.

Barzun, J. (1965) *Race: A Study in Superstition*, New York: Harper and Row (first published 1938).

BBC (1994) 'The road to Hare Krishna', *Everyman*, BBC1, 2 October.

Bell, R. and Bell, C. (1969) *City Fathers*, London: Barrie and Rockliff.

Ben-Tovim, G., Gabriel, J., Law, I. and Stredder, K. (1986) *The Local Politics of Race*, London: Macmillan.

Best Value Project Group (1997) *A Framework for Developing Best Value in Welsh Local Government*, First Report (August), Cardiff: BVPG.

Blackman, D. (1998) 'Analysing the best approach for value', *Planning*, 11 December, 11.

Blackman, T. (1991) 'Planning inquiries: a socio-legal study', *Sociology* 25: 311–27.

Blackstone, T., Parekh, B. and Sanders, P. (eds) (1998) *Race Relations in Britain*, London: Routledge.

Blair, T. (1998) *Leading the Way: A New Vision for Local Government*, London: Institute for Public Policy Research.

Blakemore, K. and Boneham, M. (1994) *Age, Race and Ethnicity*, Buckingham: Open University Press.

Blowers, A. and Pain, K. (1999) 'The unsustainable city?' in S. Pile *et al.* (eds), *Unruly Cities?*, London: Sage, 247–8.

Boyne, G. *et al.* (1999) *Best Value Service Reviews in Welsh Pilot Authorities*, Cardiff: Cardiff Business School.

Brah, A., Hickman, M.J. and Mac an Ghaill, M. (eds) (1999) *Thinking Identities: Ethnicity, Racism and Culture*, London: Macmillan.

Braithwaite, M. (1998) *Integrating Gender Equality into Local and Regional Development*, Brussels: Engender.

Brindley, T. *et al.* (1996) *Remaking Planning*, 2nd edn, London: Routledge.

Brown, C. (1984) *Black and White Britain*, London: Heinemann.

Brown, M. (1999) 'Service please', *Connections*, Spring, 10–12.

Brownill, S. and Darke, J. (1998) *Rich Mix: Inclusive Strategies for Urban Regeneration*, Bristol: Polity Press.

Brownill, S. et al. (1996) 'Local governance and the racialisation of Urban Policy in the UK: the case of urban development corporations', *Urban Studies* 33(8), 1337–55.

Brownill, S. *et al.* (1997) *Race Equality and Local Governance*, ESRC Project Paper No.3, Department of City and Regional Planning, UWCC, Cardiff.

Bulmer, M. (1996) 'The ethnic group question in the 1991 Census of population', in D. Coleman and J. Salt (eds), *Ethnicity in the 1991 Census*, vol. 1, London: HMSO.

Burawoy, M. (1985) *The Politics of Production: Factory Regimes under Capitalism and Socialism*, London: Verso.

Burgess, J.L. (1985) 'News from nowhere: the press, the riots and the myth of the inner city', in J.A. Burgess and J. Gold (eds), *Geography, the Media and Popular Culture*, London: Croom Helm.

Burns, D. *et al.* (1994) *The Politics of Decentralisation*, London: Macmillan.

Burns, W. (1963) *New Towns for Old*, London: Leonard Hill.

Cain, H. and Yuval-Davis, N. (1990) 'The equal opportunities community and the anti-racist struggle', *Critical Social Policy* 10(2): 5–26.

Carter, J. (1999) 'Ethnicity, gender and equality in the NHS', in R. Bariot, H. Bradley and S. Fentson (eds), *Ethnicity, Gender and Social Change*, London: Macmillan.

Carter, N., Brown, T., Abbott, T. and Robson, F. (1991) 'Local authorities as strategic enablers', *Planning Practice and Research* 6(2): 25–30.

Castles, A. and Miller, M. (1993) *The Age of Migration*, London: Macmillan.

Centre for Public Services (1997) *Strategy for Best Value*, Sheffield: Centre for Public Services

Chance, J. (1996) 'The Irish: invisible settlers', in C. Peach (ed.), *Ethnicity in the 1991 Census*, vol. 2, London: Office For National Statistics.

Charles, N. and Hintjens, H. (1998) 'Gender, ethnicity and cultural identity: women's "places"', in N. Charles and H. Hintjens (eds), *Gender, Ethnicity and Political Ideologies*, London: Routledge, 1–26.

Chelliah, R. (1998) *Best Value and Equal Opportunities*, London: LGIU.

Cherry, G. (1974) *The Evolution of British Town Planning*, Leighton Buzzard: Leonard Hill.

Clements, L. and Campbell, S. (1997) 'The Criminal Justice and Public Order Act and its implications for travellers', in T. Acton (ed.), *Gypsy Politics and Traveller Identity*, Hatfield: University of Hertfordshire Press.

Coates, K. and Silburn, R. (1970) *Poverty: The Forgotten Englishmen*, Harmondsworth: Penguin.

Cochrane, A. (1993) *Whatever Happened to Local Government?*, Buckingham: Open University Press.

—— (1996) 'From theories to practices: looking for local democracy in Britain', in D. King and G. Stoker (eds), *Rethinking Local Democracy*, London: Macmillan.

Cockcroft, T.W. (1995) 'Occupational culture in a South Wales police station', M.Sc. (Econ) Dissertation, Cardiff University.

Cohen, P. (1994) 'Introduction: racism in our backyard', in D. Ntolo, *The Sacred and the Profane*, Dagenham: New Ethnicities Unit, University of East London.

Coleman, D. and Salt, J. (eds) (1996) *Ethnicity in the 1991 Census Volume One*, London: HMSO.

Collinson, D.L. (1992) *Managing the Shopfloor: Subjectivity, Masculinity and Work-place Culture*, New York: de Gruyter.

Commission for Racial Equality (CRE) (1984) *Race and Council Housing in Hackney: Report of a Formal Investigation Conducted by the Commission for*

Racial Equality into the Allocation of Housing in the London Borough of Hackney, London: CRE.
—— (1991) *Employers in Cardiff, Report of a Formal Investigation*, London: CRE.
—— (1992) *Second Review of the Race Relations Act, 1976*, London: CRE.
—— (1995) *Racial Equality Means Quality*, London: CRE.
Conekin, B. (1999) ' "Here is the Modern World Itself": The Festival of Britain's representations of the future', in B. Conekin, F. Mort and C. Waters (eds), *Moments of Modernity,* London: Rivers Oram Press.
Cooper, D. (1998) *Governing Out of Order*, London: Rivers Oram Press.
Coster, G. (1992) 'Another country', *Guardian Weekend Supplement*, 1–2 June: 4–6.
Cox, H. and Morgan, D. (1973) *City Politics and the Press*, Cambridge: Cambridge University Press.
CPS (1997) *Strategy for Best Value*, Sheffield: Centre for Public Services.
CSJ (Commission for Social Justice) (1994) *Social Justice: Strategies for National Renewal*, London: Vintage.
Cullingworth, B. (ed.) (1999) *British Planning: 50 Years of Urban and Regional Policy*, London: The Athlone Press.
Dale, R. (1976) 'Work, cultures and consciousness', *People and Work, Unit 9*, Milton Keynes: Open University Press.
Damer, S. and Hague, C. (1971) 'Public participation in planning: a review', *Town Planning Review* 43(3): 219–32.
Daniels, S. (1993) *Fields of Vision*, Cambridge: Polity Press.
Davies, L. (n.d.) 'Planning for black people and ethnic minorities: a study of the south-west region', report available from the author, Faculty of the Built Environment, University of the West of England.
Davis, J. (1997) 'New Age travellers in the countryside: incomers with attitude', in P. Milbourne (ed.), *Revealing Rural 'Others'*, London: Pinter.
Davis, J., Grant, R. and Locke, A. (1994) *Out of Site, Out of Mind*, London: The Children's Society.
de Graft-Johnson, A. (1999) 'Gender, race and culture in the urban built environment', in C. Greed (ed.), *Social Town Planning*, London: Routledge.
Deakin, N. and Ungerson, C. (1973) 'Beyond the ghetto', in D. Donnison and D. Eversley (eds), *Urban Patterns, Problems and Policies*, London: Heinemann.
—— (1977) *Leaving London*, London: Heinemann.
Derounian, J. (1993) 'Facing up to rural racism', *Rural Viewpoint*, April: 1–2.
DETR (1998a) *Modernising Local Government*, London: The Stationery Office.
—— (1998b) *Modernising Local Government Improving Local Services Through Best Value*, London: The Stationery Office.
—— (1999) *Modernising Planning: A Progress Report*, London: DETR.
Dodd, V. (1999) 'Call for multi-cultural "re-branding" of Britain', *Guardian*, 8 February, 8.
Dorsett, R. (1998) *Ethnic Minorities in the Inner City*, Bristol: Policy Press.
Douglas, A. (1997) *Local Authority Sites for Travellers*, Edinburgh: The Scottish Office.
du Boulay, D. (1989) 'Involving black people in policy formulation', *Planning Practice and Research* 4(1): 13–15.
Dumbleton, B. (1977) *The Second Blitz*, Cardiff: Dumbleton.

Duncan, S. and Goodwin, M. (1988) *The Local State and Uneven Development*, London: Polity Press.

Duncan, T. (1995) 'Finding sites for travelling people', *Scottish Planning and Environmental Law* 47: 6–7.

Evans, A.C. (1995) 'Tipi or not tipi?', unpublished Diploma in Town Planning dissertation, Cardiff University.

Eversley, D. (1973) *The Planner in Society*, London: Faber and Faber.

Faludi, A. (1978) *Essays on Planning Theory and Education*, Oxford: Pergamon.

Farnsworth, R. (1989) 'Urban planning for ethnic minority groups: a review of initiatives taken by Leicester City Council', *Planning Practice and Research* 4(1): 16–22.

Flynn, N. (1997) *Public Sector Management*, London: Prentice Hall Harvester Wheatsheaf.

Forester, J. (1989) *Planning in the Face of Power*, London: University of California Press.

Franklin, B. and Passmore, J. (1998) *Developing for Diversity: The Needs of Ethnic Minority Communities*, Cardiff: Taff Housing Association.

Fraser, A. (1992) *The Gypsies*, Oxford: Blackwell.

Gabriel, J. (1994) *Racism, Culture, Markets*, London: Routledge.

Gaster, L. (1993) *Organisational Change and Political Will*, Bristol: School for Advanced Urban Studies, Bristol University.

Geddes, A. (1993) 'Asian and Afro-Caribbean representation in elected local government in England and Wales', *New Community* 20(1): 43–57.

Gibson, M. and Longstaff, M. (1982) *An Introduction to Urban Renewal*, London: Hutchinson.

Gifford, Z. (1998) 'Foreword', in S. Saggar (ed.), *Race and British Electoral Politics*, London: UCL Press, ix–xviii.

Gilg, A. and Kelly, M. (1996) 'The analysis of development control decisions', *Town Planning Review* 67(2): 203–28.

Gilroy, R. (1993) *Good Practices in Equal Opportunities*, Aldershot: Avebury.

Glaeser, A. (1998) 'Placed selves: the spatial hermeneutics of self and other in the postunification Berlin Police', *Social Identities* 4(1): 7–38.

Gleeson, B. (1999) *Geographies of Disability*, London: Routledge.

Glenny, M. (1999) 'Only in the Balkans', *London Review of Books* 21(9): 12–14.

Goss, S. (1988) *Local Labour and Local Government*, Edinburgh: Edinburgh University Press.

Green, H. (1991) *Counting Gypsies*, London: HMSO.

Greenwood, R. and Stewart, J. (eds) (1974) *Corporate Planning in English Local Government*, London: Charles Knight.

Griffith, J.A.G. (1997) *Politics of the Judiciary*, 5th edn, London: Fontana.

Griffiths, R. and Amooquaye, E. (1989) 'The place of race on the town planning agenda', *Planning Practice and Research* 4: 5–7.

Gruffudd, P. (1999) 'Prospects of Wales: contested geographical imaginations', in R. Fevre and A. Thompson (eds), *Nation, Identity and Social Theory*, Cardiff: University of Wales Press.

Hague, C. (1984) *The Development of Planning Thought*, London: Hutchinson Education.

Hall, P. *et al.* (1973) *The Containment of Urban England*, 2 vols, London: Allen and Unwin.

Hall, S. (1978) 'Racism and reaction', in Commission for Racial Equality, *Five Views of Multi-Racial Britain*, London: CRE.

—— (1986) 'Urban unrest in Britain', in J. Benyon and J. Solomos (eds), *The Roots of Urban Unrest*, Oxford: Pergamon, 45–50.

—— (1992a) 'New ethnicities', in J. Donald and A. Rattansi (eds), *'Race', Culture and Difference*, London; Sage, 39.

—— (1992b) 'The West and the rest: discourse and power', in S. Hall and B. Gieben (eds), *Formations of Modernity*, Cambridge: Polity Press.

—— (1996) *Race, The Floating Signifier*, Northampton, MA: Media Education Foundation.

Hall, S., Critcher, C., Jefferson, J., Clarke, J. and Roberts, B. (eds) (1978) *Policing the Crisis: Mugging, the State and Law and Order*, London: Macmillan.

Hambleton, R. and Thomas, H. (eds) (1995) *Urban Policy Evaluation*, London: Paul Chapman Publishing.

Hardy, D. (1991a) *From Garden Cities to New Towns*, London: E. & F.N. Spon.

—— (1991b) *From New Towns to Green Politics*, London: E. & F.N. Spon.

Hargreaves, A.G. and Leaman, J. (1995) 'Racism in contemporary Western Europe: an overview', in A.G. Hargreaves and J. Leaman (eds), *Racism, Ethnicity and Politics in Western Europe*, Aldershot: Edward Elgar.

Harrison, M.L. (1975) 'British town planning ideology and the welfare state', *Journal of Social Policy* 4: 259–74.

—— (1989) 'The urban programme, monitoring and ethnic minorities', *Local Government Studies* 15(4): 49–64.

Hartley, J. *et al.* (1995) *Managing Organisational and Cultural Change*, Luton: LMGB.

Hawes, D. (1997) *Gypsies, Travellers and the Health Service*, Bristol: Polity Press.

Healey, P. (1990) 'Policy processes in planning', *Policy and Politics* 18(1): 91–103.

Healey, P. and Underwood, J. (1978) 'Professional ideals and planning practice', *Progress in Planning* 9(2): 73–127.

Healey, P., McNamara, P., Elson, M. and Doak, A. (1982) *Land Use Planning and the Mediation of Urban Change*, Cambridge: Cambridge University Press.

Healey, P. *et al.* (eds) (1992) *Rebuilding the City*, London: E. & F.N. Spon.

Hellmann, L. (1977) 'Handicapped architecture', *Built Environment* 3(3): 216–21.

Heywood, F. and Naz, M. (1990) *Clearance: The View From the Street*, Birmingham: Community Forum.

Hickman, M. and Walter, B. (1997) *Discrimination and the Irish Community in Britain*, London: CRE.

HM Government (1998) *Memorandum to the Environment Sub-Committee of the House of Commons Environment, Transport and Regional Affairs Committee.*

Hobsbawm, E.J. (1994) *Age of Extremes: The Short Twentieth Century, 1914–1991*, London: Michael Joseph.

Home, R. (1994) 'The planner and the gypsy', in H. Thomas and V. Krishnarayan (eds), *Race Equality and Planning: Policies and Procedures*, Aldershot: Avebury.

Home Office/DETR (1998) *Managing Unauthorised Camping*, London: DETR.

House of Commons Environment, Transport and Regional Affairs Committee (1998a) *Implementing the Best Value Framework minutes of evidence, Tuesday, 2 June 1998*, London: The Stationery Office.

—— (1998b) *Implementation of the Best Value Framework. Minutes of Evidence*, HC705–iii, London: The Stationery Office.

Howard, E. (1985) *Garden Cities of Tomorrow*, Eastbourne: Attic Books.

Husband, C. (1982b) 'Introduction: "race", the continuity of a concept', in C. Husband (ed.), *'Race' in Britain: Continuity and Change*, London: Hutchinson, 11–23.

Imrie, R. (1996) *Disability and the City*, London: Paul Chapman.

Imrie, R. and Thomas, H. (1993) *British Urban Policy and the Urban Development Corporations*, London: Paul Chapman.

—— (1997) 'Law, legal structure and urban regeneration: rethinking the relationships', *Urban Studies* 34(9): 1401–18.

Jackson, P. (1987) 'The idea of "race" and the geography of racism', in P. Jackson (ed.), *Race and Racism*, London: Allen and Unwin, 3–21.

—— (1989) *Maps of Meaning*, London: Unwin Hyman.

—— (1998a) 'Domesticating the street: the contested spaces of the high street and the mall', in N.R. Fyfe (ed.), *Images of the Street: Planning, Identity and Control in Public Space*, London: Routledge, 176–91.

—— (1998b) 'Constructions of whiteness in the geographical imagination', *Area* 30(2): 99–106.

Jackson, P. and Penrose, J. (eds) (1993) *Constructions of Race, Place and Nation*, London: UCL Press.

Jacobs, J.M. (1996) *Edge of Empire*, London: Routledge.

Jay, E.S.C. (1992) *'Keep Them in Birmingham': Challenging Racism in South-West England*, London: Commission for Racial Equality.

Jeffers, S. *et al.* (1996) 'Race, ethnicity and community in three localities', *New Community* 22(1): 111–26.

Jenkins, R. (1986) *Racism and Recruitment: Managers, Organisations and Equal Opportunities in the Labour Market*, Cambridge: Cambridge University Press.

Jess, P. and Massey, D. (1995) 'The contestation of place', in D. Massey and P. Jess (eds), *A Place in the World?*, Oxford: Oxford University Press, 133–74.

Jewson, N. and Mason, D. (1986) 'The theory and practice of equal opportunities policies: liberal and radical approaches', *Sociological Review* 34(2): 307–24.

Jones, T. (1993) *Britain's Ethnic Minorities*, London: Policy Studies Institute.

Jordan, G.H. (1988) 'Images of Tiger Bay: did Howard Spring tell the truth?' *Llafur. Journal of Welsh Labour History* 5: 53–9.

Justice (1992) *Response to the Consultation Paper on the Reform of the Caravan Sites Act 1968*, London: Justice.

Kalka, I. (1991) 'The politics of community among Gujarati Hindus in London', *New Community* 17: 377–85.

Karn, V. and Phillips, D. (1998) 'Race and ethnicity in housing: a diversity of experience', in T. Blackstone, B. Parekh and P. Saunders (eds), *Race Relations in Britain*, London: Routledge, 128–57.

Katzneltson, I., Gille, K. and Weir, M. (1982) 'Race and schooling: reflections on the social basis of urban movements', in N. Fainstein and S. Fainstein (eds), *Urban Policy Under Capitalism*, London: Sage, 215–35.

Khan, V.S. (1992) 'The role of the culture of domination in structuring the experience of ethnic minorities', in C. Husband (ed.), *Race in Britain: Continuity and Change*, London: Hutchinson, 209.

Khakee, A., Somma, P. and Thomas, H. (eds) (1999) *Urban Renewal, Ethnicity and Social Exclusion in Europe*, Aldershot: Ashgate.

King, A.D. (1993) 'Cultural hegemony and capital cities', in J. Taylor *et al.* (eds), *Capital Cities*, Ottawa: Carleton University Press.

Kirklees MBC (1981) 'Mosques and madressahs', Report of the Directorate of Technical Services.

Kitchen, T. (1997) *People, Politics, Policies and Plans*, London: Paul Chapman Publishing.

Krishnarayan, V. and Thomas, H. (1993) *Ethnic Minorities and the Planning System*, London: RTPI.

Krumholz, N. and Forester, J. (1990) *Making Equity Planning Work*, Philadelphia: Temple University Press.

Le Lohé, M. (1998) 'Ethnic minority participation and representation in the British electoral system', in S. Saggar (ed.), *Race and British Electoral Politics*, London: UCL Press, 73–95.

Leach, B. (1989) 'Disabled people and the implementation of local authorities' equal opportunities policies', *Public Administration* 67(1): 65–77.

Lees, L. (1998) 'Urban renaissance and the street: spaces of control and contestation', in N.R. Fyfe (ed.), *Images of the Street: Planning, Identity and Control in Public Space*, London: Routledge, 236–53.

Leese, T. and Wareing, D. (1996) *Ethnic Communities: Communication and Environment*, Bolton: Bolton Metropolitan Borough Council.

Leicester City Council (1992) *An Appraisal of the Ethnic Monitoring of Planning Applications in Leicester, 1980–92*, Leicester: Leicester City Council.

Lester, A. (1998) 'From legislation to integration: twenty years of the Race Relations Act', in T. Blackstone, B. Parekh and P. Saunders (eds), *Race Relations in Britain* London: Routledge.

Levitas, R. (1998) *The Inclusive Society?*, Basingstoke: Macmillan.

Lewis, G. (1998) 'Introduction', in G. Lewis (ed.), *Forming Nation, Framing Welfare*, London: Routledge, 1–5.

Lewis, J. and Foord, J. (1984) 'New Towns and new gender relations in old industrial areas', *Built Environment* 10(1): 42–52.

LGMB (1993) *Fitness for Purpose*, Luton: LGMB.

LGMB/RTPI (1992) *Planning Staffs Survey 1992*, London: LGMB/RTPI.

Lister, R. (1998) 'From equality to social inclusion: New Labour and the Welfare State', *Critical Social Policy* 18(2): 215–25.

Little, J. (1999) 'Women, planning and local central relations in the UK', in T. Fenster (ed.), *Gender, Planning and Human Rights*, London: Routledge, 25–38.

Liverpool John Moores University (1998) *Feasibility Study into the Recruitment of Black and Ethnic Minorities into the Planning Profession*, London: RTPI.

Lo Piccolo, F. and Thomas, H. (n.d.) 'Legal discourse and the claim for equality in British planning', unpublished paper, available from the authors c/o Department of City and Regional Planning, Cardiff University.

Local Government Best Value Partnership (1998) *No Quality without Equality – Best Value and Equalities*, London: LGMB.

Loftman, P. and Beazley, M. (1998a) *Race, Equality and Planning*, London: LGA.

—— (1998b) *Race, Equality and Planning: Technical Survey Report*, Birmingham: Faculty of the Built Environment, UCE, Birmingham.

Lopez, L.M. and Hasso, F.S. (1998) 'Frontlines and borders: identity thresholds and Latinos and Arab American women', in J. O'Brien and J.A. Howard (eds), *Everyday Inequalities*, Oxford: Blackwell.

Lowe, P. and Goyder, J. (1983) *Environmental Groups in Politics*, London: Allen and Unwin.

MacDonald, K. (1999) 'History in the making', *Planning*, 2 July, 5.

MacEwen, M. (1994) 'Anti-discrimination law in Great Britain', *New Community* 20(3): 353–70.

Macpherson, W. (advised by T. Cook, J. Sentamu and R. Stone) (1999) *The Stephen Lawrence Inquiry: Report of an Inquiry*, Cm 4262-I, London: The Stationery Office.

—— (1999b) *The Stephen Lawrence Inquiry Appendices*, Cm 4262–II, London: The Stationery Office.

Magliocco, S. (1998) 'Playing with food: the negotiation of identity in the ethnic display event by Italian Americans in Clinton, Indiana', in B.G. Shortridge and J. Shortridge (eds), *The Taste of American Place*, Lanham, MD: Rowman and Littlefield, 145–61.

Malik, S. (1992) 'Colours of the countryside: a whiter shade of pale', *Ecos* 13(4): 33–40.

Mark-Lawson, J. and Warde, A. (1987) *Industrial Restructuring and the Transformation of a Local Political Environment: A Case Study of Lancaster*, Lancaster Regionalism Group Working Paper No.33, University of Lancaster.

Marriott, D. (1996) 'Reading black masculinities', in M. Mac an Ghaill (ed.), *Understanding Masculinities*, Buckingham: Open University Press, 185–201.

Marx, A. (1997) *Making Race and Nation*, Cambridge: Cambridge University Press.

Mason, D. (1986) 'Introduction: controversies and continuities', in J. Rex and D. Mason (eds), Theories of Race and Ethnic Relations, Cambridge: Cambridge University Press, 1–19.

—— (1990) 'Competing conceptions of fairness and the formulation and implementation of equal opportunities policies', in W. Ball and J. Solomos (eds), *Race and Local Politics*, London: Macmillan.

—— (1995) *Race and Ethnicity in Modern Britain*, Oxford: Oxford University Press.

Massey, D. *et al.* (eds) *City Worlds*, London: Routledge.

McAuslan, P. (1980) *The Ideologies of Planning Law*, Oxford: Pergamon.

McDougall, G. (1979) 'The state, capital and land: the history of town planning revisited', *International Journal of Urban and Regional Research* 3: 361–80.

McDowell, L. (1994) 'The transformation of cultural geography', in D. Gregory *et al.* (eds) *Human Geography*, London: Macmillan.

McKay, G. (1997) 'O Life unlike to ours! Go for it! New Age Travellers', in L. McDowell (ed.), *Undoing Place?*, London: Arnold, 158–70.

McLoughlin, J.B. (1973) *Control and Urban Planning*, London: Faber.

McVeigh, R. (1997) 'Theorising sedentarism: the roots of anti-nomadism', in T. Acton (ed.), *Gypsy Politics and Traveller Identity*, Hatfield: University of Hertfordshire Press.

Meller, H. (1990) 'Planning theory and women's role in the city', *Urban History Year-book* 17: 85–98.

Milbourne, P. (ed.) (1997) *Revealing Rural 'Others'*, London: Pinter.

Miles, R. (1989) *Racism*, London: Routledge.

—— (1994) 'Explaining racism in contemporary Europe', in A. Rattansi and S. Westwood (eds), *Racism, Modernity and Identity on the Western Front*, Cambridge: Polity Press.

Minister for the Regions, Regeneration and Planning (1998) *Modernising Planning: A Policy Statement*, London: DETR.

Modood, T. *et al.* (1997) *Ethnic Minorities in Britain: Diversity and Disadvantage*, London: Policy Studies Institute.

Moore, H. (1994) *A Passion for Difference: Essays in Anthropology and Gender*, Cambridge: Polity Press.

Moore, R. (1992) 'Labour and housing markets in inner city regeneration', *New Community* 18(3): 371–86.

—— (1995) review of H. Thomas and V. Krishnarayan (eds), *Race Equality and Planning*, in *Town Planning Review* 66(4): 465–6.

Morris, L. (1994) *Dangerous Classes*, London: Routledge.

Morris, R. (1998) 'Gypsies and the planning system', *Journal of Planning and Environment Law*, July: 635–43.

Munt, I. (1994) 'Race, urban policy and urban problems: a critique on current UK practice', in H. Thomas and V. Krishnarayan (eds), *Race Equality and Planning: Policies and Precedures*, Aldershot: Avebury.

Murdoch, J. and Marsden, T. (1994) *Reconstituting Rurality*, London: UCL Press.

Nadin, V. (1999) 'British planning in the European context', in B. Cullingworth (ed.), *British Planning*, London: The Athlone Press.

Nadin, V. and Jones, S. (1990) 'A profile of the profession', *The Planner* 76(3): 14–24.

Naga, R. (1999) 'Communal spaces and politics of multiple identities', reprinted in S. Pile *et al.* (eds), *Unruly Cities?*, London: Sage, 197–200.

Nallamilli, R. (1989) 'The recruitment, training and roles of black planners: a personal viewpoint', *Planning Practice and Research* 4: 26–7.

Nanton, P. (1995) 'Extending the boundaries: equal opportunities as social regulation', *Policy and Politics* 23(3): 203–12.

—— (1998) 'Community politics and the problems of partnership: ethnic minority participation in urban regeneration networks', in S. Saggar (ed.), *Race and British Electoral Politics*, London: UCL Press, 223–43.

Nayak, A. (1999) ' "Pale Warriors": skinhead culture and the embodiment of white masculinities', in A. Brah, M.J. Hickman and M. Mac an Ghaill (eds) *Thinking Identities: Ethnicity, Racism and Culture*, London: Macmillan, 71–99.

Noonan, P. (1998) 'Pathologisation and resistance: travellers, nomadism and the state', in P. Hainsworth (ed.) *Divided Society, Ethnic Minorities and Racism in Northern Ireland*, 152–83.

Oakley, J. (1997) 'Cultural ingenuity and travelling autonomy: not copying, just choosing', in T. Acton and G. Mundy (ed.), *Romani Culture and Gypsy Identity*, Hatfield: University of Hertfordshire Press.

Oatley, N. (ed.) (1998) *Cities, Economic Competition and Urban Policy*, London: Paul Chapman.

O'Brien, J. (1998) 'Introduction: differences and inequalities', in J. O'Brien and J.A. Howard (eds), *Everyday Inequalities*, Oxford: Blackwell, 1–39.

O'Brien, J. and Howard, J.A. (eds) (1998) *Everyday Inequalities* Oxford: Blackwell.

O'Leary, P. (1991) 'Anti-Irish riots in Wales', *Llafur. Journal of Welsh Labour History* 5(4): 27–36.

Ollerearnshaw, S. (1988) 'Action on equal opportunities in inner cities: the need for a policy commitment', *New Community*: 15(1): 31–46.

Omi, M. and Winant, H. (1994) *Racial Formation in the United States*, 2nd edn, London: Routledge.

Open University (1997) 'Your Place or Mine?', first broadcast 10 August.

Oppenheim, C. and Harker, L. (1996) *Poverty: The Facts*, 3rd edn, London: CPAG.

Owen, D. (1995) 'The spatial and socio-economic patterns of minority ethnic groups in Great Britain', *Scottish Geographical Magazine* 11(1): 27–35.

—— (1996) 'Size, structure and growth of the ethnic minority populations', in D. Coleman and J. Salt (eds), *Ethnicity in the 1991 Census*, vol. 1, London: HMSO.

Owen, J. (1989) 'Identifying good practice on race and planning', *Planning Practice and Research* 4: 9–12.

Pattison, S. (1998) 'Questioning values', *Health Care Analysis* 6: 352–9.

Peach, C. (1996) 'Good segregation, bad segregation', *Planning Perspectives* 11: 379–98.

—— (1996a) 'Does Britain have ghettoes?', *Transactions of the Institute of British Geographers* 21(1): 216–35.

—— (1996b) 'Introduction', in C. Peach (ed.), *Ethnicity in the 1991 Census*,

—— (1996c) 'Black-Caribbeans: class, gender and geography', in C. Peach (ed.), *Ethnicity in the 1991 Census*, vol. 2, London: HMSO.

Peach, C. (ed.) (1996d) *Ethnicity in the 1991 Census*, vol. 2, London: HMSO.

Peach, C. and Rossiter, D. (1996) 'Level and nature of spatial concentration and segregation of minority ethnic populations in Great Britain, 1991', in C. Peach (ed.), *Ethnicity in the 1991 Census*, vol. 2, London: HMSO.

Penrose, J. (1993) 'Reification in the name of change', in P. Jackson and J. Penrose (eds), *Constructions of Race, Place and Nation*, London: UCL Press.

Phillips, D. (1987) 'The rhetoric of anti-racism in public housing allocation', in P. Jackson (ed.), *Race and Racism: Essays in Social Geography*, London: Allen and Unwin.

Pile, S., Brook, C. and Mooney, G. (eds) (1999) *Unruly Cities?*, London: Routledge.

Planning Officers Society (POS) (1997) 'Initial report of the Performance Indicators Working Party', available from POS.

—— (1999) 'Getting started in best value', draft 4, mimeo.

Raban, J. (1974) *Soft City*, London: Hamish Hamilton.

Rattansi, A. and Westwood, S. (eds) (1994) *Racism, Modernity and Identity on the Western Front*, Cambridge: Polity Press.

Royal Commission on Local Government in England (1969) *Report, Vol. 1*, London: HMSO.

Platt, L. and Noble, M. (1999) *Race, Place and Poverty*, York: York Publishing Services.

Ratcliffe, P. (1984) *Racism and Reaction*, London: Routledge and Kegan Paul.

—— (1992) 'Renewal, regeneration and race: issues in urban policy', *New Community* 18(3): 387–400.

—— (ed.) (1996) *Ethnicity in the 1991 Census*, vol. 3, London: HMSO.

—— (1998) 'Planning for diversity and change', *Planning Practice and Research* 13(4): 359–69.

Rattansi, A. (1992) 'Changing the subject? Racism, culture and education', in J. Donald and A. Rattansi (eds), *'Race', Culture and Difference*, London: Sage.

Ravetz, A. (1994) 'Travelling to nowhere?', *Town and Country Planning* 63(7/8): 200–1.

Reade, E. (1987) *British Town and Country Planning*, Milton Keynes; Open University Press.

Rees, G. and Lambert, J. (1985) *Cities in Crisis*, London: Edward Arnold.

Rees, T. (1998) *More Equal Than Others?*, Cardiff: BBC Wales.

Riley, F. (1994) 'Monitoring and race equality in planning', in H. Thomas and V. Krishnarayan (eds), *Race, Equality and Planning*, Aldershot: Ashgate.

Robson, B.T. *et al.* (1994) *Assessing the Impact of Urban Policy*, London: HMSO.

Rogers, Lord (1999) 'Introduction', in Urban Task Force, *Towards an Urban Renaissance*, London: E. & F.N. Spon.

Rose, G. (1995) 'Place and identity: a sense of place', in D. Massey and P. Jess (eds), *A Place in the World?*, Oxford: Oxford University Press, 87–118.

RTPI (1996) *Planning Authorities and Racist Representations*, London: RTPI.

RTPI/CRE (1983) *Planning for a Multi-Racial Britain*, London: CRE.

Russell, H. *et al.* (1996) *City Challenge: Interim National Evaluation*, London: The Stationery Office.

Saggar, S. (1991) *Race and Public Policy*, Aldershot: Avebury.

—— (1998) 'Analyzing race and elections in British politics: some conceptual and theoretical concerns', in S. Saggar (ed.), *Race and British Electoral Politics*, London: UCL Press, 11–46.

Seabrook, J. (1993) *Victims of Development*, London: Verso.

Shuinéar, S. (1997) 'Why do Gaujos hate Gypsies so much, anyway? A case study', in T. Acton (ed.), *Gypsy Politics and Traveller Identity*, Hatfield: University of Hertfordshire Press.

Shukra, K. (1998) *The Changing Pattern of Black Politics in Britain*, London: Pluto.

Sibley, D. (1981) *Outsiders in Urban Society*, Oxford: Blackwell.

—— (1995) *Geographies of Exclusion: Society and Difference in the West*, London: Routledge.

—— (1998) 'Problematising exclusion: reflections on space, difference and knowledge', *International Planning Studies* 3(1): 93–100.

Simmie, J. (1974) *Citizens in Conflict*, London: Hutchinson.

—— (1993) *Planning at the Crossroads*, London: UCL Press.

Simpson, S. (1996) 'Non-response to the 1991 Census: the effect on the ethnic group enumeration', in D. Coleman and J. Salt (eds), *Ethnicity in the 1991 Census*, vol. 1, London: HMSO.

Skellington, R. (1996) *'Race' in Britain Today*, 2nd edn, London: Sage.

Smith, M. and Burgoyne, V. (1998) 'Different and equal', *Municipal Journal* 20 November, 22–3.

Smith, S. (1989) *The Politics of Race and Residence*, Cambridge: Polity Press.

Smith, S.J. (1985) 'News and the dissemination of fear', in J. Burgess and J. Gold (eds), *Geography, the Media and Popular Culture*, London: Croom Helm.

Solesbury, W. (1993) 'Reforming urban policy', *Policy and Politics* 21: 31–8.

Solomos, J. (1989) *Race and Racism in Contemporary Britain*, 1st edn, London: Macmillan.

—— (1993) *Race and Racism in Britain*, 2nd edn, London: Macmillan.

Solomos, J. and Back, L. (1995) *Race, Politics and Social Change*, London: Routledge.

Solomos, J. and Wrench, J. (eds) (1993) *Racism and Migration in Western Europe*, Oxford: Berg.

Spencer, S. (1998) 'The impact of immigration policy on race relations', in T. Blackstone, B. Parekh and P. Saunders (eds), *Race Relations in Britain*, London: Routledge, 74–5.

Stephenson, R. (1998) 'In what way, and to what effect is technical information used in policy making? Findings from a study of two development plans', *Planning Practice and Research* 13(3): 237–45.

Stewart, J. (1974) *The Responsive Local Authority*, London: Charles Knight & Co.

Stoker, G. and Brindley, T. (1985) 'Asian politics and housing renewal', *Policy and Politics* 13(3): 281–303.

Taylor, I., Evans, K. and Fraser, P. (1996) *The Tale of Two Cities: Global Change, Local Feeling and Everyday Life in the North of England*, London: Routledge.

Tewdwr-Jones, M. (1998) 'Planning modernised?', *Journal of Planning and Environment Law*, 519–28.

Tewdwr-Jones, M. and Harris, N. (1998) 'The New Right's commodification of planning control', in P. Allmendinger and H. Thomas (eds), *Urban Planning and the British New Right*, London: Routledge.

Thomas, H. (1979) 'An analysis of changes in planning education, 1965–75', unpublished M.Phil. thesis, University College London.

Thomas, H. (1993) 'Welsh planners voice some lingering doubts', *The Planner*, 22 October, 20–1.

—— (1994a) 'The New Right: "race" and planning in Britain in the 1990s', *Planning Practice and Research* 9(4): 353–66.

—— (1994b) 'Hot food takeaways, ethnic minorities and planning control', in H. Thomas and V. Krishnarayan (eds), *Race, Equality and Planning*, Aldershot: Avebury.

—— (1994c) 'The local press and urban renewal', *International Journal of Urban and Regional Research* 18(2), 315–33.

—— (1995) 'A model in planning consultation', *Surveyor*, 1 June, 14–15.

—— (1996) 'Public participation', in M. Tewdwr-Jones (ed.), *British Planning Policy in Transition*, London: UCL Press.

—— (1997) 'Ethnic minorities and the planning system: a study revisited', *Town Planning Review* 68(2): 195–211.

—— (1999a) 'Social town planning and the planning profession', in C.H. Greed (ed.), *Social Town Planning*, London: Routledge.

—— (1999b) 'Urban renaissance and social justice', *Town and Country Planning* 68(11): 332–3.

Thomas, H. and Imrie, R. (1993) 'What's in a name? Realignment in the politics of urban development in Cardiff', *Planet the Welsh Internationalist* 101: 8–13.

—— (1999) 'Urban policy, modernisation and the regeneration of Cardiff Bay', in R. Imrie and H. Thomas (eds), *British Urban Policy: An Evaluation of the Urban Development Corporations*, London: Sage.

Thomas, H. and Krishnarayan, V. (1994a) 'Race equality in town planning and the local authority context', *Local Government Policy Making* 21(1): 45–50.

—— (eds) (1994b) *Race Equality and Planning: Policies and Procedures*, Aldershot: Avebury.

—— (1993) 'Race, equality and planning', *The Planner* 79(3): 17–19.

Thomas, H. and Lo Piccolo, F. (1999) 'Best value, planning and race equality', paper presented at the Sheffield Planning Research Conference, March.

Thomas, H. *et al.* (1995) *Theory, Race Equality and Urban Policy Evaluation*, ESRC Project Paper No. 1, Cardiff: Department of City and Regional Planning, Cardiff University.

—— (1998) *Ethnic Minority Influence in Planning Policy*, ESRC Project Paper No. 4, Cardiff: Department of City and Regional Planning, Cardiff University.

Thomas, H., Stirling, T., Brownill, S. and Razzaque, K. (1996) 'Locality, urban governance and contested meanings of place', *Area* 186–98.

Thomas, R. (1969) *London's New Towns*, London: PEP.

Thomas, R. and Thomas, H. (1990) *'Not an Appropriate Area: The Consideration of Planning Applications for Hot Food Takeaways*, Discussion Paper on Hospitality Management no. 1, Leeds: Leeds Polytechnic.

Thornley, A. (1993) *Urban Planning Under Thatcherism*, London: Routledge.

Urban Task Force (1999a) *Urban Renaissance: Sharing the Vision*, London: Urban Task Force.

—— (1999b) *Towards an Urban Renaissance*, Final Report, London: E. & F.N. Spon.

Urry, J. (1981) *The Anatomy of Capitalist Societies*, London: Macmillan.

Verloo, M. (1994) 'Planning for public space: a gender impact assessment analysis', paper for the international conference on Women and Public Policy, December, Rotterdam.

Ward, S.V. (1994) *Planning and Urban Change*, London: PCP.

Warde, A. (1988) 'Industrial restructuring, local politics and the reproduction of labour power', *Environment and Planning, D Society and Space* 6, 75–95.

Watt, P. (1998) 'Going out of town: youth, "race" and place in the South East of England', *Society and Space* 16: 687–703.

Weber, M. (1948) 'Bureaucracy', in H.H. Gerth and C. Wright Mills (eds), *From Max Weber: Essays in Sociology*, London: Routledge and Kegan Paul, 196–244.

Welsh Office (1998a) *Local voices. Modernising Local Government in Wales*, London: The Stationery Office.

—— (1998b) *Modernising Local Government in Wales: Improving Local Services through Best Value*, London: The Stationery Office.

Wilkin, K. (1998) 'Sustainable social exclusion: the case of land-use planning and "newer" travellers', *Critical Social Policy* 18(1): 103–120.

Williams, C. (1995) 'Race and racism: some reflections on the Welsh context', *Contemporary Wales* 8: 113–31.

Williams, R. (1975) *The Country and the City*, St Albans: Paladin.

Wilson, M. (1998) *A Directory of Planning Policies for Gypsy Site Provision in England*, Bristol: Polity Press.

WLGA (1999) *Equal Opportunities Toolkit*, Cardiff: WLGA.

Wrench, J., Brar, H. and Martin, P. (1993) *Invisible Minorities: Racism in New Towns and New Contexts*, Coventry: Centre for Research in Ethnic Relations, University of Warwick.

Yinger, J.M. (1986) 'Integrating strands in the theorisation of race and ethnic relations', in J. Rex and D. Mason (eds), *Theories of Race and Ethnic Relations*, Cambridge: Cambridge University Press, 23.

Zukin, S. (1991) *Landscapes of Power*: Berkeley, CA: University of California Press.

Index

Abram, S. 93
Acton, T. 112
affirmative action *see* positive
    discrimination
Afro-Caribbeans *see* Black Caribbean
    population
agency, individual 55
Ahmad, W. 25
Ahmed, Y. 77, 91
Aldridge, M. 71
Allen, J. 120, 123, 130
Allmendinger, P. 107
Alty, R. 89
Ambrose, P. 107
Amooquaye, E. 29
Anderson, B. 118
Anthias, F. 29, 118, 119
Appadurai, A. 47n2
Areas of Outstanding Natural Beauty
    69, 116
Ashcroft, P. 70
Asians 6, 10, 11, 12, 49; leisure activities
    and space 35, 70; and new towns
    71–2; and political parties 96;
    priorities 93; town planning and 16,
    75–7; *see also* South Asians
Atkinson, R. 57, 60, 61, 62

Baber, P. 114
Back, L. 43
Bagguley, P. 38
Ball, H. 18, 62
Ball, W. 14, 95, 100
Bangladeshis 6, 7, 8, 9, 10, 11, 12; ethnic
    identity 34
Bariot, R. 28, 29
Barzun, J. 23

Beazley, M. 2, 82, 83, 84, 85, 86, 88, 89,
    92, 94, 95, 102, 110, 131
Bell, C. 65
Bell, R. 65
Ben Tovim, G. 18
Best Value regime 82, 86, 95, 97, 98–9;
    and equal opportunities 99–102; local
    planning authority responses 102–7
Bhaktivedanta Manor case 36, 46, 69,
    121
Birmingham: housing 53, 73;
    racialisation of party politics 43, 51;
    urban policy 57–8, 62–3
Black Africans 6, 7, 9, 10, 11, 12
Black Caribbean population 6, 7, 8, 9,
    10, 11, 12, 49; and political parties
    96; priorities 93
black and ethnic minority housing
    associations 53, 56–7
black people in Britain 4–12
Blackman, D. 97
Blackman, T. 46
Blackstone, T. 13
Blair, T. 62, 96, 99, 121
Blakemore, K. 29
Blowers, A. 77
Bolton: Asians' priorities 93; residential
    segregation 7
Boneham, M. 29
Booth, C. 77, 91
boundaries 3, 19, 28–9, 34, 36
Boyne, G. 101
Brah, A. 29
Braithwaite, M. 129, 130
Brindley, T. 59, 93, 94, 107
British Nationality Act (1948) 50
British Nationality Act (1981) 50
Brown, C. 49